Walt Disney's
CLASSIC MOVIE
TREASURY

A GOLDEN BOOK • NEW YORK

Western Publishing Company, Inc.,
Racine, Wisconsin 53404

Contents

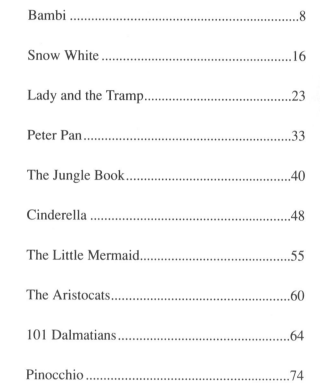

BAMBI

ambi came into the world in the middle of a thicket, one of those little hidden forest glades that seem to be open but are really screened in on all sides.

The magpie was the first to discover him. "What a beautiful child!" she cried, and she flew off through the forest to tell the news. "The young Prince is born!"

Her chattering brought dozens of birds and animals toward the thicket.

Even the owl, who had settled down for his long day's sleep, was awakened by a baby rabbit thumping at the base of his tree.

With a sigh, the owl spread his wings and flew off with the others to the thicket. There he found the squirrels and rabbits and birds peering through the undergrowth at a doe and a little spotted fawn.

The owl was the first to speak.

"This is quite an occasion," he said. "It isn't often that a young Prince is born. Congratulations!"

The doe looked up. "Thank you," she said quietly. Then she nudged her sleeping baby gently with her nose. "Wake up," she whispered. "Wake up!"

The fawn lifted his head and looked around. He looked frightened and edged closer to his mother's body. She licked him reassuringly and nudged him again. He pushed up on his thin hind legs, trying to stand. His forelegs kept crumpling, but at last they bore his weight and he stood beside his mother.

"What are you going to name the young Prince?" asked the baby rabbit.

"I'll call him Bambi," the mother answered.

"Bambi," repeated the rabbit. "That's a good name. My name's Thumper." And he hopped away with his mother and sisters.

The little fawn sank down and nestled close to his mother. She licked his spotted red coat softly.

The birds and animals slipped away through the forest, leaving the thicket in peace and quiet.

The forest was beautiful in the summer. The

trees stood still under the sky, and out of the earth came troops of flowers, unfolding their red, white, and yellow stars.

Bambi liked to follow his mother down the forest paths, so narrow that the thick, leafy bushes stroked his flanks as he passed. Sometimes a branch tripped him or a bush tangled about his legs, but always his mother walked easily and surely.

There were friends all along these forest paths. The squirrels and chipmunks looked up and called, "Good morning, young Prince." The opossums, hanging by their long tails from the branches of a tree, said, "Hello, Prince Bambi."

As Bambi and his mother reached a little clearing in the forest, they met Thumper and his family.

"Come on, Bambi," said Thumper. "Let's play."

"Yes, let's play," cried the other little rabbits, hopping over branches and hillocks and tufts of grass, dancing around the little fawn so rapidly that he looked at them in amazement.

But he soon understood and began to run on his stiff, spindly legs. He leapt over a low branch, stumbled, and fell. Thumper urged him up again, and Bambi scrambled to his feet and leapt up in the air for joy.

Thumper leapt over a fallen log and Bambi followed, but his long legs did not clear the log and he fell with a thud on top of it. As he untangled his legs and slid down on the far side of the log, he saw a family of birds on a low branch. Bambi stared at them.

"These are birds, Bambi," Thumper said. "Birds."

"Birds," said Bambi slowly. It was his first word. Bambi was pleased with himself. He repeated the word over and over to himself. When he saw a butterfly flutter across the path, he cried, "Bird, bird!" again.

"No, Bambi," said Thumper. "That's not a bird. That's a butterfly."

Bambi watched the butterfly disappear into the bushes. Then he saw a clump of yellow flowers, and he bounded toward them.

"Butterfly!" he cried.

"No, Bambi," said Thumper. "Not butterfly. Flower."

He hopped forward and pushed his nose into the flowers. Bambi did the same, pleased with the sweet smell. Suddenly he drew back. His nose had touched something furry and warm. Out from the bed of flowers came a small black head with two gleaming eyes.

"Flower!" said Bambi.

"That's not a flower," Thumper said with a giggle. "Skunk."

"Flower," said Bambi again.

"The young Prince can call me Flower if he wants to," said the skunk. "I don't mind. In fact, I like it."

Bambi had made another friend.

One morning Bambi and his mother walked down a path where the little fawn had never been before. The trail ended with a tangle of vines and bushes. A few steps more and they would be in a bright, open space. Bambi wanted to bound forward, but his mother stopped him.

"What is it?" he asked impatiently.

"It is the meadow," his mother replied.

She stood motionless, holding her head high and listening intently.

"Wait here until I call you," she said. "The meadow is not always safe. If you see me turn back, run as fast as you can."

Bambi never took his eyes off his mother as she walked out with slow, cautious steps. He saw how she listened in all directions. Then she called, "Come."

Bambi bounded out. Joy seized him and he leapt into the air three, four, five times.

"Catch me!" his mother cried, and she bounded forward. Bambi started after her. He felt as if he were flying, without any effort.

As he stopped for breath a large green frog suddenly hopped out from the clover at his feet and into a small pond. Bambi followed it and peered down at the water where it had disappeared.

As the ripples cleared he saw his own image and jumped back. Then he looked again and saw two images, side by side. He jumped again, lifted his head, and saw a small fawn standing beside him.

"Hello," she said, moving nearer to him.

Bambi backed timidly away, tripped over a root, and tumbled to the ground. He scrambled to his feet and bounded away to hide behind his mother.

"Don't be afraid, Bambi," his mother said. "That is little Faline; her mother is your Aunt Edna."

"Come and play, Bambi," Faline said, dancing toward him.

Bambi turned and dashed away as fast as he could run. Faline gave a leap and ran after him. Soon they were romping, chasing each other around bushes, and racing around hillocks.

Suddenly out of the woods came the sound of hoofbeats. Branches snapped, boughs rustled, and figures burst out of the forest. They tore by like the wind, made a wide circle on the grassy meadow and vanished into the woods again, where they could still be heard galloping.

"Who are they?" Bambi asked.

"They are the fathers," said Faline excitedly.

Out of the woods they came bursting again and suddenly stood still. Bambi stopped breathlessly to look at them. They looked like his mother and Aunt Edna, but their heads were crowned with gleaming antlers.

Then Bambi saw, standing on a rock high above the meadow, a great stag who was larger, stronger, and more dignified than all the others. Every animal stood still as the great stag slowly descended, passing the other deer without so much as a glance.

When he approached Bambi, the little fawn almost stopped breathing. The stag stopped, lowered his head, and looked searchingly at Bambi. Then he turned and walked slowly into the woods.

When he had disappeared, Bambi ran to his mother.

"That was the great Prince of the Forest," she said. "He is very brave and very wise."

"Mother, did you see?" said Bambi excitedly. "He stopped and looked at me."

Just as Bambi was about to start off to find Faline, to tell her his news, the great stag dashed back onto the meadow and uttered one dreadful word:

"MAN!"

Instantly birds and animals, crying and squawking, rushed toward the woods. As Bambi and his mother disappeared into the protection of the trees and bushes, they heard behind them on the meadow several loud, roaring noises, terrifying to Bambi's ears.

Later, as Bambi and his mother lay safely in their thicket, his mother explained. "MAN, Bambi—it was MAN in the meadow. He brings danger and death to the forest with his long stick that roars and spurts flames. Someday you will understand."

As time passed Bambi learned many things. He knew by ear the sound the field mice make, the soft tread of the pheasants, the patter of the moles. He could sniff the air and tell how things stood on the meadow.

One morning he woke up shivering with cold. His nose told him there was something strange in the world. When he looked out through the thicket, he saw everything covered with white.

"It's snow, Bambi," his mother said. "Go ahead and walk out."

Cautiously, Bambi stepped on the surface of the snow and saw his feet sink down in it. The air was calm and the sun on the white snow sparkled. Bambi was delighted.

As he walked, stepping high and carefully, a breeze shifted a branch above him ever so slightly, just enough to tip a heavy load of snow on Bambi's head. He jumped high in the air, startled and frightened, and then ran on, licking the snow from his nose. It tasted good—clean and cool.

Thumper was playing on the ice-covered pond, and Bambi trotted gingerly down the slope and out onto the smooth ice, too. His front legs shot forward, his rear legs slipped back and down he crashed! He looked up to see Thumper laughing at him.

He finally lurched to his feet and skidded across the ice dizzily, landing headfirst in a snowbank on the shore.

As he pulled himself out of the drift he and Thumper heard a faint sound of snoring. Peering down into a deep burrow they saw the little skunk lying peacefully asleep on a bed of withered flowers.

"Wake up, Flower!" Bambi called.

"Is it spring yet?" Flower asked sleepily.

"No, winter's just beginning," said Bambi.

"I'm hibernating," the little skunk said with a smile. "Flowers always sleep in the winter." And he dozed off again.

So Bambi learned about winter. It was a difficult time for all the animals in the forest. Food grew scarce. Sometimes Bambi and his mother had to strip bark from trees and eat it.

At last, when it seemed they could find no more to eat, there was a change in the air. Thin sunshine filtered through the bare branches, and the air was a little warmer. That day, too, Bambi's mother dug under the soft snow and found a few blades of pale green grass.

Bambi and his mother were nibbling at the grass when they suddenly smelled MAN. As they lifted their heads, there came a deafening roar like thunder.

"Quick, Bambi," his mother said, "run for the thicket. Don't stop, no matter what happens."

Bambi darted away and heard his mother's footsteps behind him. Then came another roar from MAN's guns. Bambi dashed among the trees in terrified speed. But when he came at last to the thicket, his mother was not in sight. He sniffed the air for her smell, listened for her hoofbeats. There was nothing!

Bambi raced out into the forest, calling wildly for his mother. Silently the great stag appeared beside him.

"Your mother can't be with you anymore," the stag said. "You must learn to walk alone."

In silence Bambi followed the great stag through the snow-filled forest.

At last it was spring. The willows shed their catkins. Everything was turning green, and the leaves looked fresh and smiling.

Bambi was standing in front of a tree, beating his new antlers against the wood to loosen the old skin that covered them.

"Stop that!" cried an irritated voice above him.

Bambi looked up and saw the owl, who sat on a branch of the tree, swaying from Bambi's blows against the trunk.

"Go away from here and let me sleep!" complained the owl. "First all the twitterpated birds are so noisy that they drive me out of my nest. Then you come along and shake me to pieces."

"Hello, Bambi," said the other deer. "Don't you remember me? I'm Faline." Bambi stared at her. Faline was now a graceful and beautiful doe.

A strange excitement swept over Bambi. When Faline trotted up and licked his face, Bambi started to dash away. But after a few steps he stopped. Faline dashed into the bushes and Bambi followed.

Suddenly Ronno, a buck with big antlers, ran from the woods and stood between Bambi and Faline.

"Stop!" he cried. "Faline is going with me."

Bambi stood still as Ronno nudged Faline down the path. He felt the blood pounding in his head. Suddenly he shot forward, Ronno turned with head lowered, and they charged together with a crash.

Ronno tossed Bambi to the ground, but he was on his feet again in a flash, charging blindly. Again and again they came together, forehead to forehead. Then Bambi braced his hind legs and hurled himself

Bambi sighed and walked off alone until he came to the pond. There on the glassy surface he saw not only his own reflection, with the fine new antlers towering above his head, but the reflection of another deer. He looked up.

on Ronno. A prong broke from Ronno's antlers, a terrific blow tore open his shoulder, and he fell to the ground, sliding down a rocky embankment.

As Ronno limped off into the forest Bambi and Faline walked away through the woods. At night they trotted onto the meadow, where they stood in the moonlight, listening to the east wind and the west wind calling to each other.

Early one morning in the autumn Bambi and Faline were asleep in the thicket. Suddenly Bambi raised his head and sniffed the air. Quietly he stepped from the thicket and went to a high cliff. There the wind brought him the scent of MAN.

As he looked the great stag came and stood beside him. "Yes, Bambi, it's MAN," he said, "a great many of them, with tents and campfires. We must go to the hills."

Bambi ran back to the thicket for Faline. But Faline had awakened at the call of the crows screaming a warning overhead. She had dashed down a path calling "Bambi! Bambi!" The fearful sounds of MAN came closer and the barking of dogs struck terror to her heart.

Bambi heard her calls and dashed toward her. He lunged at the dogs surrounding the ledge on which she stood and threw them into a whining mass.

"Jump, Faline!" Bambi called. Faline quickly jumped from the ledge and dashed into the woods.

Bambi charged furiously, then scrambled up a steep bank of loose rocks and raced through the woods.

The roar of a gun crashed almost beside him. Bambi sprang into the air and dashed blindly ahead as a killing pain shot through him and a thin burning thread ran down from his shoulder.

He stopped at last. It was comfortable just to lie there and rest.

"Up, Bambi! Get up!" The old stag was standing beside him and nudging his shoulder gently.

Bambi wanted to answer, "I can't," but something in the old stag's voice made him get up.

"Good," said the old stag. "Now come with me. The forest has caught fire from the flames of MAN's campfires. We must go to the river."

He walked swiftly ahead. Bambi followed, though he felt a terrible desire to drop to the ground. The smoke grew thicker, and he could hear the crackling roar of flames.

Other animals, large and small, were dashing through the woods, too. Now they were completely

encircled by the fire. The old stag stopped.

"The river is just beyond that wall of flames," he said. "We must go through."

They plunged into the raging fire. Smoke filled Bambi's lungs and blinded his eyes. Flames licked his sides. Then he stumbled over a rock and fell—into cool, rushing water.

Down the stream they went, over a roaring waterfall into deep water, then on again to an island in the middle of the river.

Panting and breathless, Bambi struggled onto the safe shore, already crowded with other animals. With a cry of joy Faline came running to him and gently licked the wound in his shoulder. Thumper was there, and Flower. Together the friends stood on the shore and watched the flames destroy their forest home.

Once more winter came to the forest, and the white snow covered the scars left by the fire. Then in the spring green leaves appeared, grass and flowers and wild shrubs.

Again news went through the forest, "Come along, come to the thicket. Everyone is going to see." At the thicket, the squirrels and rabbits and birds were peering through the undergrowth at Faline and two spotted fawns.

And high above them, on the cliff, where the tired old stag had bade him good-bye, Bambi stood watching—Bambi, proud father and the new great Prince of the Forest.

SNOW WHITE

Once upon a time in a faraway land, a lovely Queen sat by her window sewing. As she worked, she pricked her finger with her needle. Three drops of blood fell on the snow-white linen.

"How happy I would be if I had a little girl with lips as red as blood, skin as white as snow, and hair as black as ebony!" thought the Queen.

When spring came, her wish was granted. A little daughter was born to the Queen, and she was all her mother had desired. But the Queen's happiness was brief. Holding her baby in her arms, the Queen whispered, "Little Snow White!" and then she died.

When the lonely King married again, his new Queen was beautiful, but, alas, she was also heartless and cruel. She was jealous of all the ladies of the kingdom, but most jealous of all of the lovely little Princess.

Now the Queen's most prized possession was a magic mirror. Every day she looked into it and asked:

"Mirror, mirror on the wall,
Who is the fairest one of all?"

If the mirror replied that she was fairest in the land, all was well. But if another lady were named, the Queen flew into a furious rage and had her killed.

As the years passed Snow White grew more and more beautiful, and her sweet nature made everyone love her—everyone but the Queen.

The Queen's chief fear was that Snow White might grow to be the fairest in the land. So she banished the young Princess to the servants' quarters, made her dress in rags, and forced her to slave from morning to night.

But while she worked Snow White dreamed

16

dreams of a handsome Prince who would come someday and carry her off to his castle in the clouds. And as she dusted and scrubbed—and dreamed—Snow White grew more beautiful day by day.

At last came the day the Queen had been dreading. She asked:

> "Mirror, mirror on the wall,
> Who is the fairest one of all?"

and the mirror replied:

> "Her lips blood red, her hair like night,
> Her skin like snow, her name—Snow White!"

Pale with anger, the Queen rushed from the room and called her huntsman to her.

"Take the Princess into the forest and bring me back her heart in this jeweled box," she said.

17

The huntsman bowed his head in grief. He had no choice but to obey the cruel Queen's commands.

Snow White had no fear of the kindly huntsman. She went happily into the forest with him. It was beautiful there among the trees, and the Princess, not knowing what was in store for her, skipped along beside the huntsman, now stopping to pick violets, now singing a happy tune.

At last the poor huntsman could bear it no longer. He fell to his knees before the Princess.

"I cannot kill you, Princess," he said, "even though it is the Queen's command. Run into the forest and hide, and never return to the castle."

Then away went the huntsman. On his way back to the castle, he killed a small animal and put its heart in the jeweled box to give the wicked Queen.

Alone in the forest, Snow White wept with fright. Deeper and deeper into the woods she ran, half blinded by tears. It seemed to her that roots of trees reached up to trip her feet, that branches reached out to clutch at her dress as she passed.

At last, weak with terror, Snow White fell to the ground and lay there, sobbing her heart out.

Ever so quietly, out from burrows and nests and hollow trees, crept the little woodland animals. Bunnies and chipmunks, raccoons and squirrels gathered around to keep watch over her.

When Snow White looked up and saw them there, she smiled through her tears. At the sight of her smile, the little animals crept closer, snuggling in her lap or nestling in her arms. The birds sang their gayest melodies, and the little forest clearing was filled with joy.

"I feel ever so much better now," Snow White told her new friends. "But I still do need a place to sleep."

One of the birds chirped something, and the little animals nodded in agreement. Then off flew the birds, leading the way. The rabbits, chipmunks, and squirrels followed after, and Snow White came along with her arm around the neck of a gentle mother deer.

At last, through a tangle of brush, Snow White saw a tiny cottage nestling in a clearing up ahead.

"How sweet!" she cried. "It's just like a doll's house," and she clapped her hands in delight.

Skipping across a little bridge to the house, Snow White peeked in through one windowpane. There seemed to be no one at home, but the sink was piled high with cups and saucers and plates which looked as though they had never been washed. Dirty little

shirts and wrinkled little trousers hung over chairs, and everything was blanketed with dust.

"Maybe the children who live here have no mother," said Snow White, "and need someone to take care of them. Let's clean their house and surprise them."

So in she went, followed by her forest friends. Snow White found an old broom in the corner and swept the floor, while the little animals all did their best to help.

Then Snow White washed all the crumpled little clothes, and set a kettle of delicious soup to bubbling on the hearth.

"Now," she said to the animals, "let's see what is upstairs."

Upstairs they found seven little beds in a row.

"Why, they have their names carved on them," said Snow White. "Doc, Happy, Sneezy, Dopey—such funny names for children! Grumpy, Bashful, Sleepy! My, I'm a little sleepy myself!"

Yawning, she sank down across the little beds and fell asleep. Quietly the little animals stole away, and the birds flew out the window. All was still in the little house in the forest.

Shouldering their pickaxes, up the stairs they went—seven frightened little dwarfs.

Standing in a row at the foot of their beds, they stared at the sleeping Snow White.

"Wh-what is it?" whispered one. "It's mighty purty," said another. "Why, bless my soul, I think it's a girl!" said a third. And then Snow White woke up.

"Why, you're not children," she exclaimed. "You're little men. Let me see if I can guess your names." And she did—Doc and Bashful, Happy, Sleepy, and Sneezy, and last of all, Dopey and Grumpy, too.

"Supper is not quite ready," said Snow White. "You'll have just time to wash."

"Wash!" cried the little men with horror. They hadn't washed for, oh, it seemed hundreds of years. But out they marched when Snow White insisted. And it was worth it in the end. For such a supper they had never before tasted. Nor had they ever had such an evening of fun. All the forest folk gathered around the cottage windows to watch them play and dance and sing.

"Hi ho, hi ho,
It's home from work we go—"

Seven little men came marching through the woods, singing on their way. As they came in sight of their cottage, they stopped short. Smoke was curling from the chimney, and the door was standing open!

"Look! Someone's in our house!"

"Maybe a ghost—er a goblin—er a demon!"

"I knew it," said one, with a grumpy look. "Been warning you for two hundred years something awful was about to happen!"

At last, on timid tiptoe, in they went.

"Someone's stolen our dishes," growled the grumpy one.

"No, they're hidden in the cupboard," said Happy, with a grin. "But, hey! My cup's been washed! Sugar's all gone!"

At that moment a sound came from upstairs. It was Snow White yawning and turning in her sleep.

"It's up there—the goblin—er demon—er ghost!"

Meanwhile, back at the castle, the huntsman presented to the wicked Queen the box which, she thought, held Snow White's heart.

"Aha!" she gloated. "At last!" And down the castle corridors she hurried, straight to her magic mirror.

> *"Now, magic mirror on the wall,*
> *Who is the fairest one of all?"*

she asked.

But the honest mirror replied:

> *"With the seven dwarfs she'll spend the night,*
> *The fairest in the land, Snow White."*

Then the Queen realized that the huntsman had tricked her. She flung the jeweled box at the mirror, shattering the glass into a thousand pieces. Then, shaking with rage, the Queen hurried down to a dark cave below the palace where she worked her Black Magic.

First she disguised herself as a toothless old woman dressed in tattered rags. Then she searched her books of magic spells for a horrid spell to work on Snow White.

"What shall it be?" she muttered to herself. "The poisoned apple, the Sleeping Death? Perfect!"

In a great kettle she stirred up a poison brew.

Then she dipped an apple into it—one, two, three times—and the apple came out a beautiful rosy red, the most tempting apple you could hope to see.

Cackling with wicked pleasure, the Queen dropped her poisoned apple into a basket of fruit and started on her journey to the home of the seven dwarfs.

She felt certain that her plan would succeed, for the magic spell of the Sleeping Death could be broken only by Love's First Kiss, and the Queen was certain no lover would find Snow White, asleep in that great forest.

It was morning when the Queen reached the great forest, close to the dwarfs' cottage. From her hiding place she saw Snow White saying good-bye to the seven little men as they marched off to work.

"Now be careful!" they warned her. "Watch out for the Queen." And Snow White promised that she would.

But when a poor, ragged old woman with a basket of apples appeared outside her window, Snow White never thought to be afraid. She gave the old woman a drink of water and spoke to her kindly.

"Thank you, my dear," the Queen cackled. "Now in return won't you have one of my beautiful apples?" And she held out to Snow White the poisoned fruit.

Down swooped the little birds and animals, pecking and clawing at the wicked Queen. But still Snow White did not understand. "Stop it!" she cried. "Shame on you." Then she took the poisoned apple and bit into it, and fell down lifeless on the cottage floor.

Away went the frantic birds and animals into the woods to warn the seven dwarfs. Now the dwarfs had decided not to do their regular jobs that day. They were hard at work making a gift for Snow White to tell her of their love.

They looked up in surprise as the birds and animals crowded around them. At first they did not understand. Then they realized that Snow White must be in danger. "The Queen!" they cried, and they ran for home.

They were too late. They came racing into the clearing just in time to see the Queen slide away into the shadows. They chased her through the

gloomy woods until she plunged into a bottomless gulf and disappeared forever. But that did not bring Snow White back to life.

When the dwarfs came home, they found Snow White lying as if asleep. They built her a bed of crystal and gold, and set it up in the forest. There they kept watch, night and day.

After a time a handsome Prince of a nearby kingdom heard travelers tell of the lovely Princess asleep in the forest, and he rode there to see her. At once he knew that he loved her truly, so he knelt beside her and kissed her lips.

At the touch of Love's First Kiss, Snow White awoke. There, bending over her, was the Prince of her dreams. Snow White knew that she loved him, too. She said good-bye to the seven dwarfs and rode off with the Prince to his Castle of Dreams Come True.

LADY AND THE TRAMP

It was on Christmas Eve that Lady came to live with her People, Jim Dear and Darling. They loved her at once, but as often happens they needed some training from her.

For example, they thought she would like a little bed and blankets of her own. It took some howls and whining on Lady's part to show them their mistake. But it was not long before they understood that her place was at the foot of Jim Dear's bed—or Darling's in her turn. People are really quite intelligent, as every dog knows. It just takes a little patience to make them understand.

By the time spring rolled around, Lady had everything under control. Every morning she wakened Jim Dear with a bark and a lick at his hand. She brought his slippers and stood by until he got up.

Then out she raced, through her own small swinging door, to meet the postman at the gate. After the postman came the paperboy; and then it was breakfast time. Lady sat beside Jim Dear and Darling to make certain that not a bite or a crumb happened to go to waste.

After making certain that Darling did not need her help with the housework, Lady went out to circle the house to keep all danger away. She barked at sparrows and dragonflies in a brave and fearless way.

Then she was free to visit around. Lady had two close friends of her own, who lived in the houses on either side of hers. One was an old Scottish Terrier, known to his friends as Jock. The other was a fine old Southern gentleman, Trusty by name. Trusty was a bloodhound, and in the old days he'd had one of the keenest noses south of the Mason-Dixon Line. The three spent many happy days together.

Perhaps the nicest part of the day came at the end. That was when Jim Dear came home. Lady would race to meet him at his whistle, and scamper home at his side. It took only a moment to reach the little house, and then the family was together again, just the three of them—Jim Dear, Darling, and Lady.

And all this added up to making her the happiest dog in the world.

It was autumn of that year when a bit of urgent business brought a stranger to the neighborhood. The stranger was a cocky young mongrel known around the town simply as "The Tramp." This day he was two jumps ahead of the dogcatcher's net, rounding the corner near Lady's house. Just then along the street came a stately open carriage,

followed by two proud carriage hounds. The Tramp fell in step with the two proud hounds until the dogcatcher gave up the chase and ambled away.

"Understand the pickings are pretty slim around here, eh? A lid on every trash can, a fence around every tree," he had just said, when he saw, from the corner of one twinkling eye, the dogcatcher wandering away. "Oh, oh!" he barked, and dropped out of step—no marching to someone else's tune for him!

"Well," he thought, with a merry cock of his head, "I may as well have a look around as long as I'm here and my time's my own."

And his feet led him down the shady street to the house where Lady lived.

Poor Lady was in a sad state when he appeared. The first dark shadow had fallen over her life.

"Why, Miss Lady," Trusty asked her, "is something wrong?"

"Well, Jim Dear wouldn't play when I went to meet him—and then he called me That Dog!" Lady admitted sadly.

"That Dog!" cried Jock. He and Trusty were shocked. But they tried to make light of it.

"I wouldn't worry my wee head about it," Jock told her as cheerily as he could. "Remember, they're only humans, after all."

"Yes, I try," said Lady with tears in her dark eyes. "But Darling—we've always enjoyed our afternoon romps together, but yesterday she wouldn't go out for a walk at all, and when I picked up a soft ball she dropped, and got ready for a game, she said, 'Drop that, Lady!' And she struck me— yes, she did."

To Lady's surprise, Jock and Trusty were laughing now.

"Don't take it too seriously," Jock explained. "Don't you see, Lassie, Darling's expecting a wee bairn?"

"Bairn?" said Lady.

"He means a baby, Miss Lady," Trusty said.

"What's a baby?" Lady wanted to know just as the Tramp came along.

"Well," said Jock, staring thoughtfully, "they resemble humans, only they're smaller. They walk on all fours—"

"And if I remember correctly," Trusty broke in, "they beller a lot."

"They're very expensive," Jock warned her. "You'd not be permitted to play with it."

"But they're mighty sweet," smiled Trusty.

"And very, very soft," said Jock.

"Just a cute little bundle of trouble," a new voice broke in. It was the Tramp, who swaggered up to join the group. "They scratch, pinch, pull ears," he went on to say, "but any dog can take that. It's what they do to your happy home! Homewreckers, that's what they are! Just you wait, Miss, until Junior gets here.

"You get the urge for a nice, comfortable scratch, and—'Put that dog out,' they say. 'She'll get fleas on the baby.'

"You start barking at a strange mutt, and—'Stop that racket,' they say. 'You'll wake up the baby.'

"No more of those nice, juicy cuts of beef. Leftover baby food for you!

"Instead of your nice, warm bed by the fire—a leaky doghouse in the rain!"

"Oh, dear!" sobbed Lady.

Jock rushed to her side. "Don't you listen, Lassie," he growled. "No Human is that cruel."

"Of course not, Miss Lady," Trusty put in. "Everyone knows, a dog's best friend is his Human!"

"Ha, ha," laughed the Tramp as he turned to leave. "Just remember this, pigeon. A Human's heart has only just so much room for love and affection, and when a baby moves in—the dog moves out!"

Poor Lady! She had a long time to worry—all through the long, dreary winter months. At last, in the spring, on a night of wind and rain, in a most confusing flurry, the baby came.

Now there was a stranger in Lady's old room. Lady was scarcely allowed inside the door. And when she did follow Darling in, all she could see was a small high bed, and a strange wrapped-up shape in Darling's arms. But there was a smile on Darling's lips, and a softness in Darling's eyes. When she spoke, she spoke softly, and often sang small songs. So Lady began to think the baby must indeed be something sweet—if only they could be friends and play! Perhaps it might have worked out that way soon, if only Jim Dear had not been called away!

"I'll only be gone a few days," Jim Dear explained to Lady, with an old-time pat on the head. "Aunt Sarah will be here to help you, and I'm counting on you to—"

Knock! Knock!

The door shook under a torrent of bangs. It was Aunt Sarah. Lady watched from between Jim Dear's legs as a stern-faced lady marched in, leaving a stack

of luggage on the doorstep for Jim Dear to bring in.

"I'll put your bags away for you, Aunt Sarah," Jim Dear offered. But she pushed him back.

"No need for that, James. You just skedaddle or you'll miss your train."

"Oh—er, all right, Aunt Sarah," Jim Dear said. But he managed a last pat for Lady at the door. "It's going to be a little rough for a while," she understood from his pat. "But it won't be long, and remember, Lady, I'm depending on you to watch over things while I'm away."

Then Jim Dear was gone, quite gone.

Lady knew her job. She raced upstairs, to the bed where Darling was having her afternoon rest. And Lady snuggled down on the coverlet, within patting distance of her hand.

Not for long, though!

"What is that animal doing here?" Lady heard Aunt Sarah's voice.

"Oh, it's just Lady," Darling said with a smile.

"Get off that bed," snapped Aunt Sarah—and she pushed. "You'll get fleas on the baby! Shoo!"

Poor Lady! She was hustled straight out of the room, back down to the front hall. There, still waiting, stood Aunt Sarah's bags, so she gave them an experimental sniff.

There was something peculiar about one basket— an odor Lady did not understand. She sniffed again. She circled the basket. Zip! Out shot a silken paw and clawed her from behind!

Lady pounced on the basket—and out shot two forms! Yes, two Siamese cats. They were sly, they were sleek, they were tricky as could be.

They walked across the mantelpiece, scratched the best table legs, they bounced on the pillows Lady never touched—but whenever Aunt Sarah came into the room, they made it seem that Lady had done everything bad, and they had been twin angels!

"Get away, little beast!" Aunt Sarah would say, kicking at Lady with a toe. "Poor darlings," she would coo, scooping up the cats in her arms. "Dogs don't belong in the house with you!"

Poor Lady! She was blamed for trying to catch the goldfish, when really she was just protecting them from the cats. And when the cats opened the

canary cage and were chasing the poor frightened little thing—it was Lady who was blamed by Aunt Sarah, of course, and put out at night in the rain! Everything was just as the Tramp had said. Oh, what a sad, sad life!

The worst day of all was still to come. That was the day Aunt Sarah took Lady to the pet shop and bought her a muzzle!

"It isn't safe to have this beast unmuzzled with a

baby in the house," she said. Tears filled poor Lady's eyes. Then the muzzle was snapped on. "There now, you little brute!" said Aunt Sarah.

Lady could stand no more. She reared back on her strong little legs until her leash snapped. And away ran Lady.

She had never been alone in the city. The crowds frightened her, as did the clatter of hurrying wheels. Down a dim and quiet alley she ran, and she found a hiding place behind a big barrel. There she lay and shook with fright.

"Well, pigeon, what are you doing here?" she heard a brisk voice ask.

It was the Tramp, and how handsome he looked to Lady, how big and strong! She snuggled her head on his manly chest and had herself a good cry.

"There, there," he said in a gentler tone. "Get it out of your system and then tell me what this is all about."

So Lady told him the whole sad story.

"And I don't know what to do next," she told him with a sob.

"First of all we've got to get rid of that catcher's mitt," said the Tramp with a nod at her muzzle. "Let's see—a knife? No, that's for humans. A scissors? A saw? Teeth! That's what we need. Come on, we'll visit the zoo."

Lady had never heard of a zoo, but she trustingly followed along, and did just as the Tramp told her to, until they were safely past the No Dogs sign, strolling down the sunny paths inside.

The paths were lined with high fences, and beyond the fences—well, never in her wildest dreams had Lady imagined that animals came in such a variety of sizes and shapes and colors. But though all of them were nice about it, there did not seem to be one who could help—until they came to the Beaver House.

"Say," said Tramp, "if ever a fellow was built to cut, it's Beaver. Let's call on him." So they did.

"That's a pretty cute gadget," Beaver said, pointing at Lady's muzzle. "Make it yourself?"

"Oh, no," said Lady.

"We were hoping you could help us get it off," the Tramp explained.

"Get it off? Hmm, let's have a look at it. No, I'm afraid not. The only way I can get it off is to chew through it, and that seems a shame..."

"That's exactly what we had in mind," the Tramp said with a grin.

"It is?" The Beaver was surprised. "Well, it's your thingamajig. Hold still now. This may hurt a bit."

Lady held as still as could be.

"There!" said Beaver. And with a smile he handed her the muzzle. She was free.

"It's off! It's off!" cried Lady, bouncing up and down the paths with joy. "Oh, thank you, thank you," she stopped to say as the Tramp prepared to lead her off.

"Here!" said the Beaver. "You're forgetting something—your gadget."

"Keep it if you wish," said the Tramp with a lordly air.

"I can?" marveled Beaver. "Well, say, thanks." And as they looked back he was trying it on with a happy smile.

"The question is, what do you want to do now, pigeon?" the Tramp asked as they left the zoo behind.

"Oh, I'll have to go home now," Lady said.

"Home?" said the Tramp. "You go home now and you'll just be sliding your head into another muzzle. Stay away a few hours, let them worry a little. Have dinner with me at a little place I know, and then I'll show you the town."

Lady had never known anyone so charming. She

found herself following along. And she had to admit that dinner on the back step of a little restaurant was the best meal she'd had for weeks. Then they went to the circus—Lady's first; they had wonderful seats under the first row.

After that, they took a stroll in the park, and since the night was warm, and they were young, time passed all too quickly. The first rays of morning caught Lady by surprise.

"Oh, dear," she said. "I must go home."

"Look," said Tramp, "they've given you a pretty rough time. You don't owe them a thing. Look at the big wide world down here. It's ours for the taking, pigeon. What do you say?"

"It sounds wonderful," Lady admitted, "but it leaves out just one thing—a baby I promised to watch over and protect."

The Tramp gave a deep sigh.

"You win," he said. "I'll take you home."

But on the way they passed a chicken yard. Tramp could not resist.

"Ever chase chickens? No? You've never lived." He was scraping a hole under the fence.

"But we shouldn't," said Lady.

"That's why it's fun," the Tramp explained.

So she followed him in; and when the chickens squawked and the farmer came running, it was Lady who was caught. Oh, the Tramp tried to warn her, but she simply didn't know her way around. The next thing she knew, she was in the Dog Pound!

Lady had never met dogs like those she found in the Pound. At first they frightened her. But she soon found they had hearts of gold—and she found they knew the Tramp.

"Now there's a bloke what never gets caught!" said one.

"Yup, his only weakness is dames," said another. "Got a new one every week."

"He does?" said Lady. "Well, I certainly hope I wouldn't give a second thought to a person like that!" But really she felt very sad. She was sure now the Tramp had let her be caught so he could go on to another "dame."

Her reception when she got home did not make her feel any better. She was put out in the doghouse on a stout chain!

When the Tramp came around to call next day, Lady would not even speak to him. That was just what one stranger in the yard had hoped to see. That stranger was slinking silently along under the cover of the tall grass near the fence. From the end of the fence it was a short dash to the shelter of the woodpile. And there he lurked, waiting for the darkness—that archenemy of all society, the rat!

The rat was no stranger in one way. He had often poked around this house, trying to find a way in. But always he had been frightened off by the thought of a dog on guard.

Now, seeing Lady safely chained far from the back door, and having watched her send the Tramp away, the rat thought his big chance had come at last!

So in the dim light of dusk, he left his hiding place and scurried toward the back door.

Lady was standing at her doghouse doorway—looking sadly after the Tramp, and wondering if she had been too cruel not to let him try to explain—when she saw it—that sly, evil figure slinking toward her house—toward Darling and the baby!

Lady had never seen a rat before, but some

instinct told her that this creature was evil and vicious. It must not be allowed in the house!

When she saw it slinking through her own little swinging door, Lady went wild with rage! Barking wildly, she lunged against the chain. Far down the street, the Tramp heard her and stopped in his tracks.

Upstairs in the house, Aunt Sarah heard, too, but she was not one to understand.

"Lady! Stop that racket!" she snapped, then slammed the window and turned away.

Darling heard the uproar. "What is it, Aunt Sarah?" she asked.

"Nothing, Elizabeth, but that spoiled brat carrying on because she's chained up."

"But she's never carried on like this before," Darling worried. "Could someone be trying to break in? Perhaps if we went down to see?"

"Nonsense," snapped Aunt Sarah. "Stop being ridiculous and go back to sleep, Elizabeth. And you—hush up, you little beast!"

At that very moment the evil rat was pulling himself, step by step, up the stairs.

But at that moment, too, the Tramp came back.

"What's wrong, pigeon!" he asked.

"A horrible creature—went in the house," Lady panted anxiously.

"Horrible creature? Sure you're not seeing things?"

"Oh, please, please!" cried Lady. "Don't you understand? The baby—we must protect the baby!"

With one last lunge she snapped the chain; staggering forward, she broke into a run, and raced fearlessly for the back door.

The Tramp was close behind her. "Take it easy," he told her in his firm, soothing tones, "remember, I'm right with you."

Through the kitchen they raced, side by side in the darkness, then into the hall and up the stairs. Lady led the way to the baby's room; but just inside the door they both stopped short, for there, sure enough, was the rat!

The Tramp knew what to do, and he wasted no time. He disposed of the rat behind a chair in the corner, while Lady stood guard over the crib.

The Tramp was just returning, still panting from his battle, when Aunt Sarah, broom in hand, appeared. "Take that, you mangy cur!" she cried, lowering the broom on the Tramp.

He winced and ran before the weapon—and found himself locked in a dark closet!

Now Darling was there, too, cuddling the baby.

"Lady," she said in surprise, "whatever got into you?"

"Humph!" said Aunt Sarah. "It's plain enough. She's jealous of the baby and brought one of her vicious friends in to attack the child."

"Oh, I'm sure not," cried Darling. "I believe that she saw the stray and came in to protect the baby."

"Rubbish!" said Aunt Sarah. "But Lady is your responsibility. If you don't know your duty, I know mine. Tomorrow I notify the authorities. They'll take care of this other brute once and for all. And as for you"—she picked Lady up by the scruff of her neck—"I'm locking you in the kitchen for the night."

Bad news travels fast in the animal world. By morning everybody in the neighborhood knew— every pigeon, canary, and squirrel—that the Tramp had been picked up and was to be taken off to be executed. Aunt Sarah's cats knew, and for once even they felt something like sympathy as they tiptoed past the kitchen where Lady sobbed alone.

Jock and Trusty heard it; they watched from behind the shrubbery as the Dog Pound wagon stopped at the door, and the catcher came out, leading the Tramp to his doom.

"We misjudged him badly," Jock admitted.

"Yes," said Trusty. "He's a very brave lad. And Miss Lady's taking it very hard."

"There must be some way we can help," said Jock. But they could not think what it would be.

Lady knew, though, there was just one chance. And it came when a taxi stopped at the door. Jim Dear was home at last!

Darling told him the story of their terrible night.

"But I still don't understand," said Jim. "Why should a strange dog—and Lady—?"

Lady, leaping at the kitchen door, tried to say that she could explain.

Jim Dear opened the door and knelt beside her while she jumped up to lick his face.

"Lady, what's all this about, old girl? You know the answer, I'm sure," he said.

For reply Lady jumped past him and raced up the stairs.

"She's trying to tell us something," Darling cried.

Jim Dear was at Lady's heels.

"You're right, dear," he said. And when Lady showed him the dead rat behind the chair, at last he knew what it was.

"Don't you see?" he cried. "That strange dog wasn't attacking the baby. He was helping Lady protect it instead."

"Oh, Jim Dear, and we've sent him to be—" Darling wailed, clasping her hands.

"I don't see the reason for all this fuss," Aunt Sarah said sternly.

"Aunt Sarah," said Jim. "I'm going to save that dog. And when I come home, I trust that you will be ready to leave."

"Well, I never!" Aunt Sarah gasped.

Then off raced Jim Dear in the taxicab, on the trail of the Dog Pound wagon. But Lady was ahead of him. With Trusty and Jock beside her, she was off through the town on the wagon's trail.

They made some wrong turns. There were some dead ends. But at last they sighted the wagon ahead, with the Tramp watching them through the wire mesh.

Straight to the horse's feet the three dogs ran. Then, barking and snapping and leaping about, they set the horse to rearing nervously until the whole wagon swayed and tipped! They had won!

Now up rattled Jim Dear's taxicab.

"That dog," cried Jim Dear, pointing to the Tramp, who was rubbing noses with Lady through the mesh. "It's all been a terrible mistake."

"You mean he's yours, Mister?" the driver said.

"Yes," said Jim Dear. "He's mine."

So home they all went, in a taxi with Jim Dear. And that was the end of the story—almost.

Let us visit that little house once more, at merry Christmastime. See the Baby playing on the floor, surrounded by wiggling puppy dogs. Jim Dear and Darling are watching Baby, with love and pride in their eyes. And watching the puppies every bit as proudly—are Lady and the Tramp.

PETER PAN

In a quiet street in London lived the Darling family. There were Father and Mother Darling, and Wendy, Michael, and John. There was also the children's nursemaid, Nana—a St. Bernard dog.

For Nana and the children the best hour of the day was bedtime, for then they were together in the nursery. There Wendy told wonderful stories about Peter Pan of Never Land. This Never Land was a magical spot with Indians and mermaids and fairies—and wicked pirates, too.

John and Michael liked best of all to play pirate. They had some fine, slashing duels between Peter Pan and his archenemy, the pirate Captain Hook.

Father Darling did not like this kind of play. He blamed it on Wendy's stories of Peter Pan, and he did not approve of those stories, either.

"It is time for Wendy to grow up," he decided. "This is your last night in the nursery, Wendy girl."

All the children were very upset by that. Without Wendy in the nursery there would be no more stories of Peter Pan! Then to make matters worse, Father Darling became annoyed with Nana and decided the children were too old to be treated like puppies. So he tied Nana in the garden for the night.

When Mother and Father Darling had gone out for the evening, leaving the children snug in their beds with Nana on guard below, who should come to the nursery but Peter Pan! It seemed he had been flying in from Never Land to listen to the bedtime stories, all unseen. Only Nana had caught sight of him once and nipped off his shadow as he escaped. So back he came, looking for his lost shadow and hoping for a story about himself. With him was a fairy, Tinker Bell. When Peter heard that Wendy was to be moved from the nursery, he hit upon a plan. "I'll take you to Never Land with me, to tell stories to my Lost Boys!" he decided as Wendy sewed his shadow back on.

Wendy thought that was a lovely idea—if Michael and John could go, too. So Peter Pan taught them all to fly—with happy thoughts and faith and trust, and a sprinkling of Tinker Bell's pixie dust. Then out the nursery window they sailed, heading for Never Land, while Nana barked frantically below.

Back in Never Land, on the pirate ship, Captain Hook as usual was grumbling about Peter Pan. You see, once in a fair fight long ago, Peter Pan had cut off one of the pirate captain's hands, so he had to wear a hook instead. Then Pan threw the hand to a crocodile, who had enjoyed the taste of Hook so much that he had been lurking around ever since, hoping to nibble at the rest of him. Fortunately for the pirate, the crocodile had also swallowed a clock. He went "tick-tock" when he came near, which gave a warning to Captain Hook.

Now, as Captain Hook grumbled about his young enemy, there was a call from the crow's nest.

"Peter Pan ahoy!"

"What? Where?" shouted Hook, twirling his spyglass around the sky. "Swoggle me eyes, it *is* Pan!" Hook gloated. "Pipe up the crew...Man the guns...We'll get him this time at last!"

"Oh, Peter, it's just as I've dreamed it would be—Mermaid Lagoon and all," Wendy was saying when the first of the pirates' cannonballs ripped through the cloud close beside their feet and went sizzling on past.

"Look out!" cried Pan. "Tinker Bell, take Wendy and the boys to the island. I'll stay here and draw Hook's fire."

Away flew Tinker Bell, as fast as she could go. In her naughty little heart she hoped the children would fall behind and be lost. She was especially jealous of the Wendy girl, who seemed to have won Peter Pan's heart.

Straight through the Never Land jungle flew Tinker Bell, down into a clearing beside an old dead

tree called Hangman's Tree. She landed on a toadstool, bounced to a shiny leaf, and pop! a secret door opened for her in the knot of the hollow tree.

Zip! Down a slippery tunnel Tinker Bell slid. She landed at the bottom in an underground room—the secret house of Peter Pan.

Ting-a-ling! she tinkled, flitting about from one corner of the room to the next. She was trying to awaken the sleeping Lost Boys, who lay like so many curled-up balls of fur.

At last, rather grumpily, they woke up and stretched in their little fur suits. And they listened to Tinker Bell.

"What? Pan wants us to shoot down a terrible Wendy bird? Lead us to it!" they shouted, and out they hurried.

But then Peter Pan arrived. How angry he was when he discovered that the boys had tried to shoot down Wendy, even though he had caught her before she could be hurt.

"I brought her to be a mother to us all and to tell us stories," he said.

"Come on, Wendy," said Peter, "I'll show you the mermaids. Boys, take Michael and John to hunt some Indians."

So Peter and Wendy flew away, and the boys marched off through the forest, planning to capture some Indians. There were wild animals all around,

but the boys never thought to be afraid, and not a creature harmed them.

"First we'll surround the Indians," John decided. "Then we'll take them by surprise."

John's plan worked splendidly, but it was the Indians who used it. Disguised as moving trees, they quietly surrounded the boys and took *them* by surprise!

Soon, bound with ropes, the row of boys marched away, led by the Indians to their village on the cliff.

"Don't worry, the Indians are our friends," the Lost Boys said, but the chief looked stern.

Meanwhile, on the other side of the island, Wendy and Peter were visiting the mermaids in their peaceful Mermaid Lagoon. As they were

When Wendy and Michael and John appeared, flying wearily, the Lost Boys tried to pelt them with stones and sticks—especially the "Wendy bird." Down tumbled Wendy, all her happy thoughts destroyed—for without them no one can fly.

"Hurray! We got the Wendy bird!" the Lost Boys shouted.

When Peter and Wendy brought Tiger Lily home, the chief set all the captives free. Then what a wonderful feast they had! All the boys did Indian dances, and learned wild Indian chants, and Peter Pan was made a chief! Only Wendy had no fun at all, for she had to help the squaws carry firewood.

"I've had enough of Never Land," she thought grumpily. "I'm ready to go home right now!"

While the Indian celebration was at its height, Smee, the pirate, crept up through the underbrush and captured Tinker Bell.

Trapped in his cap, she struggled and kicked, but Smee took her back to the pirate ship and presented her to Captain Hook.

"Ah, Miss Bell," said Hook sympathetically, "I've heard how badly Peter Pan has treated you since that scheming girl Wendy came. How nice it would be if we could kidnap her and take her off to sea to scrub the decks and cook for the pirate crew!"

Tinker Bell tinkled happily at the thought.

"But, alas," sighed Hook, "we don't know where Pan's house is, so we cannot get rid of Wendy for you."

Tinker Bell thought this over. "You won't hurt Peter?" she asked, in solemn tones.

"Of course not!" promised Hook.

Then she marched to a map of Never Land and traced a path to Peter's hidden house.

"Thank you, my dear," said wicked Captain Hook, and he locked her up in a lantern cage, while he went off to capture Peter Pan!

That night when Wendy tucked the children into their beds in the underground house, she talked to them about home and mother. Soon they were all so homesick that they wanted to leave at once for home. Wendy invited all the Lost Boys to come and live with the Darling family. Only Peter refused to go. He simply looked the other way as Wendy and the boys told him good-bye and climbed the tunnel to Hangman's Tree.

Up in the woods near Hangman's Tree waited Hook and his pirate band. As each boy came out, a hand was clapped over his mouth and he was quickly tied up with ropes. Last of all came Wendy.

chatting together Peter suddenly said, "Hush!"

A boat from the pirate ship was going by. In it were wicked Captain Hook and Smee, the pirate cook. And at the stern, all bound with ropes, sat Princess Tiger Lily, daughter of the Indian chief.

"We'll make her talk," sneered Captain Hook.

"She'll tell us where Peter Pan lives, or we'll leave her tied to slippery Skull Rock, where the tide will wash over her." But proud and loyal Tiger Lily would not say a single word.

Peter and Wendy flew to Skull Rock. Peter, by imitating Hook's voice, tried to trick Smee into setting Tiger Lily free. That almost worked, but Hook discovered the trick, and came after Peter with his sword. Then what a thrilling duel they had, all over that rocky cave where Princess Tiger Lily sat, with the tide up to her chin!

Peter won the duel and rescued Tiger Lily just in the nick of time. Then away he flew to the Indian village, to see the Princess safely home. And Wendy came along behind.

Zip, zip, she was bound up, too, and the crew marched off with their load of children, back to the pirate ship.

"Blast it!" muttered Captain Hook. "We still don't have Pan!"

So he and Smee left a bomb, wrapped as a gift from Wendy, for poor Peter to find. Very soon, they hoped, Peter would open it and blow himself straight out of Never Land.

Imagine how terrible Tinker Bell felt when she saw all the prisoners, and knew it was her fault!

The children were given a terrible choice: turning pirates or walking the plank. To the boys the life of a pirate sounded fine, sad to say, and they were all ready to join up. But Wendy was shocked at that. "Never!" she cried.

"Very well," said Hook. "Then you shall be the first to walk the plank, my dear."

Everyone felt so terrible—though Wendy was ever so brave—that no one noticed when Tinker Bell escaped and flew off to warn Peter Pan.

What a dreadful moment when Wendy said good-bye and bravely walked out the long, narrow plank that led to the churning sea!

And then she disappeared. Everyone listened, breathless, waiting for a splash, but not a sign of one came! What could the silence mean?

Then they heard a familiar, happy crow. It was Peter Pan in the rigging, high above. Warned by Tinker Bell, he had come just in time to scoop up Wendy in midair and fly with her to safety.

"This time you have gone too far, Hook," Peter cried.

He swooped down from the rigging, all set for a duel. And what a duel it was!

While they fought, Tinker Bell slashed the ropes that bound the boys and they forced the pirates into jumping overboard and rowing away in their boat.

Then Peter knocked Hook's sword overboard, and Hook jumped, too. When the children last saw the wicked Captain Hook, he was swimming for the boat, with the crocodile tick-tocking hungrily behind him.

Peter Pan took command of the pirate ship. "Heave those halyards. Up with the jib. We're sailing for London," he cried.

"Oh, Michael! John!" cried Wendy. "We're going home!"

And sure enough, with happy thoughts and faith and trust, and a liberal sprinkling of pixie dust, away flew that pirate ship through the skies till the gangplank was run out to the Darlings' nursery windowsill.

But now that they had arrived, the Lost Boys did not want to stay. "We've sort of decided to stick with Pan," they said.

So Wendy, John, and Michael waved good-bye as Peter Pan's ship sailed off through the sky, taking the Lost Boys home to Never Land, where they still live today.

THE JUNGLE BOOK

Baloo the bear came down the forest trail one bright and beautiful day. He was singing of honey and bees and pawpaw trees and other things that bears like. Baloo often sang, for he was a happy and lighthearted creature. Some of the other animals in the Indian jungle said he was lightheaded, too. This did not bother Baloo. He was a very large bear, and while size does not quite take the place of wisdom, it helps. Even Kaa the mighty python slithered to one side when Baloo came bumbling along.

Baloo rounded a turn in the path and stopped and blinked. "Well," said he, "what have we here?"

The small boy who sat scratching at the ground with a twig did not even look up.

"I believe it's a man-cub!" said Baloo. He bent and sniffed at the boy in a friendly fashion.

"You leave me alone!" cried the man-cub. He got up and aimed a puny punch at Baloo's midsection.

"Pitiful!" said Baloo. "Boy, you need help. Want old Baloo to teach you to fight like a bear?"

The boy stopped scowling. His big dark eyes grew wide. "Would you?" he asked.

"Sure. First, give me a growl. Scare me."

The man-cub bared his teeth and growled. As growls went in that part of the woods, it amounted to nothing at all.

"Um!" said Baloo. He didn't want to hurt the man-cub's feelings. "We could try a little footwork," he suggested brightly.

The man-cub clenched his fists and danced back and forth in front of Baloo. He darted in under the bear's arms and punched. He missed. Baloo swung a huge paw and the man-cub went sprawling.

"Fine teacher you are," said a chilly voice.

The bear looked around. Bagheera, the prim and proper black panther, sat watching. "Tell me," said Bagheera, "if you knock your pupil senseless, how do you expect him to remember the lesson?"

Baloo frowned. He was not fond of Bagheera. The panther was forever asking awkward questions.

The man-cub scrambled to his feet. "I'm not hurt," he insisted. "I'm tough!"

"You're all right, boy," said Baloo. "Say, what do they call you?"

"He is Mowgli," announced Bagheera.

"Mowgli?" Baloo cocked his head to one side and looked at the man-cub with real interest. He had, of course, heard of Mowgli. All the jungle animals knew his story. Mowgli was the human baby who had been found abandoned beside a stream. The wolf pack had adopted him and raised him as their own.

"I'm taking him to the man-village," said Bagheera. "The wolf pack has decided that he must return to his own people."

Baloo was horrified. "But they'll ruin him. They'll make a man out of him!"

"I want to stay in the jungle," Mowgli protested.

"Of course you do," said Baloo.

"And just how would he survive in the jungle?" asked stuffy old Bagheera.

It was another of those awkward questions, but this time Baloo was ready. A wonderful idea had bloomed in his mind. He would adopt Mowgli. The man-cub would make a great bear. "I'll take care of him," said Baloo. "I'll teach him all I know."

"That shouldn't take long," snorted Bagheera.

Baloo wasn't listening. Nor was Mowgli. First, said Baloo, Mowgli was not to worry. In the jungle, there was nothing to worry about. Coconuts and bananas and pawpaws grew everywhere. Bees hummed on every side, making honey just for the jungle folk. And one could always pick up a handful of tasty ants. What more could a bear want?

Mowgli wasn't sure about the ants, but he was fond of bananas and pawpaws and honey. "I'm going to like being a bear," he said.

"You bet you are," Baloo agreed. "This is really the life." He let his legs fold under him so that he slid down a little bank into a river that flowed slowly past.

"Hah!" said the panther. "Well, don't just sit there. We have to get the man-cub back!"

Baloo looked up into the green and empty treetops. "How do we do that?" he wondered.

Bagheera thought about it for a moment. "They'll take him to their king," he said. "They'll take him to those old ruins."

"The hidden city?" said Baloo. "But we never go there."

"We'd better go now if we want to see Mowgli again," said Bagheera.

Mowgli slid into the river, too. It felt good.

Baloo scooped Mowgli out of the water and set the man-cub high and dry on his furry stomach. The two floated peacefully along.

"You're going to make one swell bear," said Baloo.

Then, so quickly that Baloo did not even see it happen, Mowgli disappeared.

"Baloo!" The scream came from high overhead.

Baloo splashed out of the stream. He looked up and he felt himself go cold. A band of chattering, gibbering monkeys had snatched Mowgli. Now they clung to the topmost branches of the trees and they tossed the man-cub from hand to hand.

"Give me back my man-cub!" yelled Baloo.

"Come and get him!" jeered one of the monkeys, and he pelted Baloo with fruit.

"Baloo! Help me!" shouted Mowgli.

The rain of fruit stopped and the monkeys fled through the trees, taking the man-cub with them.

"What happened?" Bagheera the panther had heard the man-cub scream and had come running along the riverbank. "Where's Mowgli?" he demanded.

"Those mangy monkeys," said Baloo miserably. "They carried him off."

The two animals set out toward the forbidden place where once men had piled stones upon stones to make palaces and temples. Long ago the men had left the city. Trees had pushed into the courtyards. Vines had climbed up over the walls.

No respectable animal ever went to the ruined city. But the ape king, who was more than a little mad, held his court there. He ruled his empty-headed band of monkeys from a man-thing called a throne. It stood in a weed-choked garden beside a building which had once been a palace.

It was sunset when Baloo and Bagheera arrived at the old city. They made not a sound as they stole up to a place where a banyan tree had tumbled stones down from a wall.

"There he is," whispered Bagheera.

Baloo looked through the gap in the wall. He saw the ape king crouched on his throne. He saw the glittering eyes of hundreds of monkeys. And he saw Mowgli. The man-cub squatted on one arm of the throne and stared at the ape king.

"I hear, man-cub, that you want to stay in the jungle," the ape king was saying.

"Yes," answered Mowgli. "Yes, I do."

"Well, I can fix it for you," offered the ape king. "We're cousins, after all. I walk like you. I talk like you. I want to be a man, man-cub. All I need is the secret."

"Secret?" said Mowgli.

"Tell me how to make the red flower," said the ape king.

"The red flower? Fire? But I don't know how to make fire."

"That scoundrel!" exclaimed Bagheera. "So that's what he's after."

Baloo was deeply shocked. Every right-thinking animal feared and shunned man's red flower.

"We must be quick," Bagheera decided. "Baloo, you create a disturbance, and I'll rescue Mowgli."

"Yes, sir!" said Baloo. He loved to create disturbances.

Beyond the broken wall, the ape king crooned of man's red fire. His hundreds of subjects crooned, too, and then they began to dance.

"What a beat!" murmured Baloo. He liked music. "I'm gone, man—gone!"

And he *was* gone, right through the break in the wall. "Oh, no!" moaned Bagheera as the bear joined the dancing monkeys and stamped and swayed to their music.

The ape king looked around. At first he thought he had a very large ape among his subjects. Then he looked more closely.

"Baloo!" shouted the ape king.

"Baloo!" cried Mowgli. "It's you!"

Baloo seized Mowgli and ran. Unfortunately, the bear had no time to plot a course. Instead of making for the gap in the stone wall, he dodged down into one of the dark corridors of the old palace.

"After him!" shrieked the ape king.

Baloo stumbled through blackness, hearing the sounds of small monkey feet scurrying behind him. There was a shrill monkey scream and a deep cat growl, and Baloo knew that Bagheera was near him.

There were more screams and more growls. Baloo sped out of the dark corridor into a room where wide windows let in the twilight. The ape king darted in from one side and Mowgli was snatched away from Baloo.

"Give me my man-cub!" snarled Baloo. He lumbered after the ape, and brushed against a huge pillar. Stones rumbled and scraped and slid.

"My city!" yelped the ape king.

Stones groaned and crumbled and fell.

The ape king dropped Mowgli, and Baloo picked up the man-cub.

A wall buckled and came crashing down.

Bagheera was beside Baloo. "This way!" he said.

The bear, the panther, and the man-cub raced out through the shattered wall. They ran into the cool jungle night. They did not stop until the cries of the monkeys had faded behind them.

Mowgli slept that night beneath a huge tree, and Bagheera and Baloo kept watch. The bear dozed from time to time, but just before dawn, the panther roused him.

"What is it?" asked the bear.

"Baloo, you can't adopt Mowgli," said Bagheera. "He has to go back to the man-village."

"Oh, stop worrying, Bagheera," said the bear. "I'll take care of him."

"You can't," said Bagheera. "Shere Khan the tiger is returning to this part of the jungle. The ravens brought news of it two days ago. That's why the wolf pack sent Mowgli away."

"Shere Khan?" Baloo was puzzled. "What's he got to do with Mowgli?"

"He hates man with a vengeance. You know that. He fears man's gun and man's fire."

"But Mowgli doesn't have a gun, or fire."

"Shere Khan won't wait until he does," said the panther. "He'll get Mowgli while he's young and helpless. And you won't be able to stop him."

Baloo looked at the panther in silent misery. He knew Bagheera was right. He was a large bear, but he was no match for the tiger.

"You must do what's best for the boy," said Bagheera. "Make Mowgli go to the man-village."

The sky was pink with morning. "Wake Mowgli

44

now and tell him," urged Bagheera.

Baloo shivered and sighed, but he did wake Mowgli. And told him.

"But you said I could be a bear!" cried Mowgli. "You're just like Bagheera!" Mowgli turned and disappeared into the underbrush.

Again the bear and the panther joined forces to hunt for the man-cub. They followed Mowgli's scent through the jungle until they came to a stream. Mowgli's footprints went down into the water. They did not appear again on the other side.

"I'll take to the trees," said Bagheera. "Maybe I can spot him from there. You search the riverbank. He probably came out downstream."

Bagheera darted up a tree trunk while Baloo nosed along the bank. Sure enough, not a mile had the bear gone before he found the footprints. But this time Baloo saw a second set of tracks. A giant cat had come this way, following close behind the man-cub. Shere Khan was on Mowgli's trail!

Baloo considered bellowing for Bagheera, but there was no time for talk. The bear began to run.

The sky darkened as Baloo forced his way through dense thickets. Mowgli must have raced in panic; his heels had dug hard into the earth of the jungle floor. He had crossed several paths, but he had not turned onto any of them.

Purple-black storm clouds hung low in the sky when Baloo came to a place where the jungle ended and a barren plain stretched ahead. Beside a black pool stood a blasted, lifeless tree. Mowgli was there, facing his enemy, Shere Khan.

"Run, Mowgli!" yelled Baloo, and the bear threw himself forward and caught the tiger by the tail.

Shere Khan gasped and roared with rage. His great paw went up.

At that instant there was a deafening clap of thunder. Lightning split the sky and darted down to sear the shriveled tree stump. The tiger struck, and pain exploded in Baloo's head.

The bear knew nothing for a time. Then he knew that he was lying on the ground and his head hurt very badly. And it was raining.

"Bagheera?" Mowgli spoke softly. "Bagheera, what's the matter with Baloo?"

The man-cub was alive. Baloo felt a great joy. Still, he was not quite ready to open his eyes.

"You must be brave," said Bagheera the panther. "You must be as brave as Baloo was."

"Oh, Bagheera!" cried Mowgli.

"When great deeds are remembered in this jungle, one name will stand above all others," said the panther. "The name of our friend Baloo the bear."

Baloo opened one eye and peeked. Mowgli knelt beside him. Tears and rain were running down his face. Bagheera sat like a solemn statue. "This spot where Baloo fell will be a hallowed place," said Bagheera.

Baloo opened both his eyes and chuckled his deepest chuckle. "Don't stop, Baggy," he coaxed. "You're doing great!"

"You four-flusher!" scolded Bagheera. The panther was mightily irritated. He had delivered a beautiful oration in praise of a dear, departed friend, only to have the friend pop up grinning and chortling.

"Baloo! Baloo, you're alive!" Mowgli hurled himself at the bear. "You're all right!"

"Never felt better." This was not quite true. Baloo sat up stiffly and rubbed his head. "What happened to old stripes?" he wanted to know.

"Shere Khan?" said Bagheera. "Mowgli drove him away."

"Is that the truth? Say, boy, you're really all right!"

"Mowgli is a man after all," said Bagheera. "He used man's weapon." The panther nodded toward the tree stump. It sizzled in the rain and wisps of smoke curled up from it. "Lightning struck that dead tree," said Bagheera. "The red flower bloomed there. Mowgli took a blazing branch and the tiger fled. I saw it. Shere Khan will never come back to this part of the jungle."

"That's my boy!" laughed Baloo. He gave the man-cub a big bear hug.

"Now I can stay with you, Baloo," said Mowgli.

"You bet you can," said Baloo.

Bagheera looked pained. He was a most orderly panther, and he liked things in their proper places. Surely the man-village was the proper place for a man-cub. However, Mowgli had defeated the dreaded Shere Khan. Bagheera could argue no more.

"The man-cub has earned the right to stay," admitted Bagheera. A crafty look stole across the panther's face. "It seems rather a shame," he said. "We've come very close to the man-village. Would you like to see it, Mowgli?"

"See it?"

"It's quite interesting," said Bagheera. "We won't go in, of course, or show ourselves in any way. We can just look from the edge of the jungle."

"Well," said Mowgli, "as long as we don't go in."

He and Baloo followed Bagheera back into the jungle and along a trail to a place where a brook bubbled over some stones and splashed into a clear little pool. Beyond the brook was a meadow, and beyond the meadow was a fence made of stakes. Mowgli saw thatched roofs inside the fence. Smoke drifted up. "The red flower blooms in the man-village," said Mowgli.

"Always," replied Bagheera.

A gate in the fence swung open, and a little girl came out and walked across the meadow. She had a jug balanced on her head.

"What's that?" asked Mowgli.

"It's a girl-cub," said Bagheera quietly.

"Forget about those," warned Baloo. "They're nothing but trouble."

"I want a better look," said Mowgli. He shinnied up a tree that grew next to the pool.

The girl-cub reached the pool and bent to fill her jug. Mowgli edged out onto a branch, the better to see her. There was a brisk crack. The branch split and Mowgli tumbled down into the pool.

The little girl was not a whit upset. She giggled. Mowgli got up and took a step or two toward her— whereupon she dropped the jug.

"Don't do it," breathed Baloo.

But Mowgli did it. He picked up the jug and held it out to the girl-cub. She did not take it. Instead, she turned and walked back toward the man-village. After a short, bewildered moment, Mowgli put the jug on his own head and walked after her. At the village gate he paused. Then he followed the girl inside.

"It had to happen, Baloo," said Bagheera. "Mowgli is among his own people, where he belongs."

The panther and the bear turned from the man-village. Poor Baloo felt completely bereft. But it was

not possible for the bear to grieve for very long. The sun had come out and it was warm in the clearings. Baloo began to sing of pawpaw trees and mangoes and other things dear to the heart of a bear. But when he and Bagheera came to a fork in the trail, and the panther stopped to take his leave, Baloo made a last protest.

"I still think he'd have made one swell bear!" said Baloo.

The panther nodded. "He would have made a most admirable bear."

Bagheera did not believe that, but he smiled to himself as he padded off. He could afford to be generous with Baloo. After all, he had had his own way.

CINDERELLA

Once upon a time in a far-off land, there lived a kindly gentleman. He had a fine home and a lovely little daughter, and he gave her all that money could buy—a horse of her own, a funny puppy dog, and beautiful dresses to wear.

But the little girl had no mother. She did wish for a mother and for other children to play with. So her father married a woman with two daughters. Now, with a new mother and sisters, he thought, his little daughter had everything to make her happy.

But alas! the kindly gentleman soon died. His fine home fell into disrepair. And his second wife was harsh and cold. She cared only for her own two

ugly daughters. To her lovely stepdaughter she was cruel as cruel could be.

Everyone called the stepdaughter "Cinderella" now. For she had to work hard, she was dressed in rags, and she sat by the cinders to keep herself warm. Her horse grew old, locked up in the barn. And her dog was not allowed in the house.

But do you suppose Cinderella was sad? Not a bit! She made friends with the birds who flew to her windowsill. She made friends with the barnyard chickens and geese. And her best friends of all were—guess who—the mice!

The musty old house was full of mice. Their homes were in the garret, where Cinderella lived. She made little clothes for them, and gave them all names. And they thought Cinderella was the sweetest and most beautiful girl in the world.

Every morning her friends the mice and birds woke Cinderella from her dreams. Then it was breakfast time for the household—with Cinderella doing all the work, of course. Out on the back steps she set a bowl of milk for the stepmother's disagreeable cat, who watched for his chance to catch the mice. The faithful dog had a tasty bone.

There was grain for the chickens and ducks and geese. And Cinderella gave some grain to the mice—when they were out of reach of the cat, of course. Then back into the house she went.

Up the stairway she carried breakfast trays for her stepmother and her two lazy stepsisters. And down she came with a basket of mending, some clothes to wash, and a long list of jobs to do for the day.

"Now let me see," her stepmother would say. "You can clean the large carpet in the main hall. And wash all the windows, upstairs and down. Scrub the terrace. Sweep the stairs—and then you may rest."

"Oh," said Cinderella. "Yes." And off to work she went.

Now across the town from Cinderella's home was the palace of the King. And in the King's study one day sat the King himself, giving orders to the Great Grand Duke. "The Prince must marry!" said the King. "It is high time!"

"But, Your Majesty, what can we do?" asked the Duke. "First he must fall in love."

"We can arrange that," said the King. "We shall give a great ball, this very night, and invite every girl in the land!"

There was great excitement in Cinderella's home when the invitations to the King's ball came.

"How delightful!" the stepsisters said to each other. "We are going to the palace to a ball!"

"And I—" said Cinderella, "I am invited, too!"

"Oh, you!" laughed the stepsisters.

"Yes, you!" mocked the stepmother. "Of course you may go, if you finish your work," she said. "And if you have something suitable to wear. I said IF." And she smiled a horrid smile.

Cinderella worked as hard as she could, all the long day. But when it was time to leave for the ball, she had not had a moment to fix herself up, or to give a thought to a dress.

"Why, Cinderella, you are not ready," said her stepmother when the coach was at the door.

"No. I am not going," said Cinderella sadly.

"Not going! Oh, what a shame!" the stepmother said with her mocking smile. "But there will be other balls."

Poor Cinderella! She went to her room and sank sadly down, with her head in her hands.

But a twittering sound soon made her turn around.

Her little friends had not forgotten her. They had

been scampering and flying about, as busy as could be, fixing a party dress for her to wear.

"Oh, how lovely!" she cried. "I can't thank you enough," she told all the birds and the mice. She looked out the window. The coach was still there. So she started to dress for the ball.

"Wait!" cried Cinderella. "I am coming, too!"

She ran down the long stairway just as the stepmother was giving her daughters some last commands. They turned and stared.

"My beads!" cried one stepsister.

"And my ribbon!" cried the other, snatching off Cinderella's sash. "And those bows! You thief! Those are mine!"

So they pulled and they ripped and they tore at the dress, until Cinderella was in rags once more. And then they flounced off to the ball.

Poor Cinderella! She ran to the garden behind the house. And there she sank down on a low stone bench and wept as if her heart would break.

But soon she felt someone beside her. She looked up, and through her tears she saw a sweet-faced woman. "Oh," said Cinderella. "Good evening. Who are you?"

"I am your fairy godmother," said the little woman. And from the thin air she pulled a magic

wand. "Now dry your tears. You can't go to the ball looking like that!

"Let's see now, the first thing you will need is—a pumpkin!" the fairy godmother went on.

Cinderella did not understand, but she brought the pumpkin.

"And now for the magic words! Salaga doola, menchika boola—bibbidi, bobbidi, boo!"

Slowly, up reared the pumpkin on its pumpkin vine, and it turned into a handsome magic coach.

"What we need next is some fine, big—mice!"

Cinderella brought her friends, the mice. And at the touch of the wand they turned into prancing horses.

Then the old horse became a fine coachman.

And Bruno the dog turned into a footman at the touch of the wand and a "Bibbidi, bobbidi, boo!"

"There," said the fairy godmother, "now hop in, child. You've no time to waste. The magic only lasts till midnight!"

"But my dress—" Cinderella looked at her rags.

"Good heavens, child!" laughed the fairy godmother. "Of course you can't go in that! Bibbidi, bobbidi, boo!"

The wand waved again, and there stood

Cinderella wearing the most beautiful gown in the world and tiny slippers of glass.

The Prince's ball had started. The palace was blazing with lights. The ballroom gleamed with silks and jewels. And the Prince smiled and bowed, but still looked bored as all the young ladies of the kingdom in turn curtsied before him.

Up above on a balcony stood the King and the Duke, looking on. "Whatever is the matter with the Prince?" cried the King. "He doesn't seem to care for one of those beautiful maidens."

"I feared as much," the Duke said with a sigh. "The Prince is not one to fall in love at first sight."

But just at that moment he did! For at that moment Cinderella appeared at the doorway of the ballroom. The Prince caught sight of her through the crowd. And like one in a dream he walked to her side and offered her his arm.

Quickly the King beckoned to the musicians, and they struck up a dreamy waltz. The Prince and Cinderella swirled off in the dance. And the King, chuckling over the success of his plan to find a bride for the Prince, went happily off to bed.

All evening the Prince never left Cinderella's side. They danced every dance. They ate supper together. And Cinderella had such a wonderful time that she quite forgot the fairy godmother's warning until the clock in the palace tower began to strike midnight. *Bong! Bong!* the clock struck.

"Oh!" cried Cinderella. The magic was about to end!

Without a word she ran from the ballroom, down the long palace hall, and out the door. One of her little glass slippers flew off, but she could not stop.

She leapt into her coach, and away they raced for home. But as they rounded the first corner the clock finished its strokes. The spell was broken. And there in the street stood an old horse, a dog, and a ragged girl staring at a small round pumpkin. About them some mice ran chattering.

"Glass slipper!" the mice cried. "Glass slipper." And Cinderella looked down. Soon enough, there was a glass slipper on the pavement.

"Oh, thank you, godmother!" she said.

Next morning there was great excitement in the palace. The King was furious when he found that the Duke had let the beautiful girl slip away.

"All we could find was this one glass slipper," the Duke admitted. "And now the Prince says he must marry the girl whom this slipper fits. And he will not marry anyone else."

"He did?" cried the King. "He said he would marry her? Well then, find her! Scour the kingdom, but find that girl!"

All day and all night the Duke with his servant traveled about the kingdom trying to find a foot on which the glass slipper would fit. In the morning, his coach drove up before Cinderella's house.

The news of the search had run on ahead, and the stepmother was busy rousing her ugly daughters and preparing them to greet the Duke. For she was determined that one of them should wear the slipper and be the Prince's bride.

"The Prince's bride!" whispered Cinderella. "I must dress, too. The Duke must not find me like this."

Cinderella went off to her room to dress, humming a waltzing tune. Then the stepmother suspected the truth—that Cinderella was the girl the Prince was seeking—and would marry! So the stepmother followed Cinderella—to lock her in her room.

The mice chattered a warning, but Cinderella did not hear them—she was off in a world of dreams.

Then she heard the key click. The door was locked.

"Please let me out—oh, please!" she cried. But the wicked stepmother only laughed and went away.

"We will save you!" said the loyal mice. "We will somehow get that key!"

The household was in a flurry. The Grand Duke had arrived. His servant held the glass slipper.

"It is mine!" "It is mine!" both stepsisters cried.

And each strained and pushed and tried to force her foot into the tiny glass slipper. But they failed.

Meanwhile, the mice had made themselves into a long, live chain. The mouse at the end dropped down into the stepmother's pocket. He popped up

again with the key to Cinderella's room! At once the mice hurried off with the key.

Now the Grand Duke was at the door, about to leave. Suddenly, down the stairs Cinderella came flying.

"Oh, wait, wait please!" she called. "May I try the slipper on?"

"Of course," said the Duke. And he called back the servant with the slipper. But the wicked

stepmother tripped the boy. Away sailed the slipper, and crash! it splintered into a thousand pieces. "Oh my, oh my!" said the Duke. "What can I ever tell the King?"

"Never mind," said Cinderella. "I have the other here." And she pulled from her pocket the other glass slipper!

So off to the palace went Cinderella in the King's own coach, with the happy Grand Duke by her side. The Prince was delighted to see her again. And so was his father, the King. So was everyone. For this sweet and beautiful girl won the hearts of all who met her.

In no time at all she was Princess of the land. And she and her husband, the charming Prince, rode to their palace in a golden coach to live happily ever after!

THE LITTLE MERMAID

Triton, the great Sea King, had seven lovely daughters. The youngest, whose name was Ariel, worried her father deeply. Though King Triton had warned her never to visit the world above the water's surface, Ariel often disobeyed him.

Ariel and her friend Flounder liked to visit Scuttle the sea gull. Scuttle would tell them all about the human objects that Ariel discovered in wrecked ships at the bottom of the sea.

One day, when Triton found out that Ariel had been visiting above the water again, the Sea King grew angry. He was so worried about his daughter's safety that he asked his trusted friend Sebastian the crab to watch over Ariel.

A few days later Ariel noticed a ship sailing overhead, on the surface of the sea. "Human beings!" said Ariel, swimming quickly toward the ship. Sebastian and Flounder swam after her.

When Ariel reached the ship, she saw a handsome young sailor whom the other sailors called Prince Eric. It was love at first sight!

Suddenly the sky darkened. Heavy rain began to fall and lightning split the sky. Prince Eric's ship was no match for the terrible storm, and soon the prince was thrown overboard.

"I've got to save him!" thought Ariel. She struggled to pull the drowning prince up onto the beach. Prince Eric did not stir as Ariel gently touched his face and sang him a beautiful love song. Ariel then kissed the prince and dove back into the sea.

Prince Eric awoke to find Sir Grimsby, his loyal steward, at his side. "A wonderful girl saved me," said the still-dazed prince. "She sang to me in the most beautiful voice I have ever heard. I want to find that girl and marry her!" Prince Eric, too, had fallen in love.

King Triton was furious when he discovered that his youngest daughter had fallen in love with a human being. He rushed to the cave where his disobedient child kept her collection of human treasures.

The little mermaid tried to reason with her father. "Daddy, I love him so!" she cried. "I want to be with him."

"NEVER!" Triton shouted. "He's a human being. A fish-eater!" The Sea King raised his magic trident angrily and destroyed all of Ariel's human treasures. Then the mighty Sea King left.

Ariel buried her face in her hands and wept. "Leave me alone," she sobbed when Sebastian and Flounder tried to comfort her.

Meanwhile, nearby, evil forces were at work. Ursula, a wicked Sea Witch who had ruled the kingdom before Triton, was looking for a way to regain power. She could see Ariel crying in her crystal ball, and an idea came to her. "I shall destroy the Sea King through his daughter," she said excitedly.

Ursula sent her slimy eel servants, Flotsam and Jetsam, to Ariel's cave. They convinced the little mermaid that Ursula could help her to win her beloved prince's love. Ariel ignored Sebastian's warnings and swam off with Flotsam and Jetsam to meet the Sea Witch.

"I have a deal for you, my sweet child," began

Ursula when Ariel entered the witch's lair.

"A deal?" asked Ariel innocently.

"Yes," said the witch. "I will make you human for three whole days. If you can get the prince to

kiss you before the sun sets on the third day, you will be able to stay with him forever, as a human being. But, if he does not kiss you, then you will turn back into a mermaid...and you will belong to me!

"The price for this favor," the witch continued, "is your *voice*!"

"My voice?" asked Ariel in shock. "But then I won't be able to talk or sing. How will I get the prince to fall in love with me?"

"You still have your pretty face," replied Ursula. "It should be easy."

Ariel agreed to Ursula's deal and the Sea Witch cast her magic spell. An amazing change took place. Ariel lost her tail, grew legs, and became entirely human. At the same time, her voice flew from her body and was captured inside a seashell.

When she went to find the prince, Ariel was helped ashore by Sebastian, Scuttle, and Flounder, who still watched over their friend. She tried to speak to them, but no sound came.

Soon Ariel saw Prince Eric. He had been lovesick over her ever since he had heard her sing. At first the prince was sure Ariel was the girl who had rescued him, but when he learned that she couldn't speak, he thought he must be wrong.

Prince Eric felt sorry for Ariel, who seemed lost and all alone. He took her back to his palace.

During the next two days Prince Eric grew fond of Ariel. On a boat ride together, Eric was about to kiss Ariel when Flotsam and Jetsam overturned the boat.

On the morning of the third day there was great excitement throughout the kingdom. Prince Eric was going to marry a young maiden he had just met! Unfortunately for Ariel, Eric was now under a spell. Using her magic, Ursula had disguised herself as a lovely young girl. And because she spoke with Ariel's voice—which she carried in a seashell worn around her neck—Eric believed that she was the girl who had saved him from drowning. Poor Ariel was heartbroken.

The wedding was to take place on a special wedding ship. Scuttle the sea gull flew over it just as the bride was passing in front of a mirror. Scuttle saw that her reflection was that of the Sea Witch! He rushed off to tell Ariel and her two loyal friends.

Sebastian quickly formed a plan. Flounder would help Ariel get to Eric's ship, and Scuttle would arrange for some of his friends to delay the wedding.

"I'm going to tell Triton about all this," said Sebastian.

Prince Eric and the maiden were standing at the altar about to be married when a flock of sea gulls swooped down. Scuttle pulled the seashell containing Ariel's voice from around the Sea Witch's neck. The shell shattered, and Ariel's voice returned to Ariel, who had just climbed on board.

"Oh, Eric, I love you," said Ariel.

Suddenly a harpoon struck Ursula's shoulder. Prince Eric had come to rescue Ariel. The little mermaid swam to the surface with him. But Ursula followed close behind, growing bigger and angrier, until she rose out of the water.

Prince Eric swam to his ship and climbed on board. He grabbed the wheel and turned the prow toward Ursula. The Sea Witch was about to fire a deadly bolt from the trident at Ariel, when the prince's vessel slammed into Ursula, destroying the evil witch.

Now that Ursula was dead, Triton was free. He rose from the sea, his trident back in hand. He could see Ariel watching over Prince Eric, who was lying on the shore, unconscious.

"She really does love him, doesn't she?" the Sea King asked.

Sebastian, who was nearby, nodded.

"I shall miss her," Triton said. Then he raised his trident and shot a magic bolt at Ariel's tail.

At once, the little mermaid's tail disappeared, and she was human once again. Prince Eric awoke to see his beloved Ariel standing beside him on the shore. He kissed her and soon they were married. Prince Eric and Ariel sailed off together, and they lived happily ever after.

"Then it *was* you all along!" said the delighted Prince. But just as they were about to kiss, the sun disappeared over the horizon. Ariel's three days were up and she was changed back into a mermaid. The Sea Witch had triumphed after all. Ursula grabbed Ariel and dove off the ship.

Thanks to Sebastian's warning, Triton was waiting at Ursula's lair. "I'll let your daughter go," cried Ursula, "but only in exchange for you!" Triton agreed, and he became Ursula's prisoner. She now had his magic trident and controlled the undersea kingdom.

THE ARISTOCATS

Thomas O'Malley, the alley cat, was on his way to Paris. O'Malley was enjoying himself, as he usually did. He liked broad boulevards, but he also liked narrow alleys. He liked mornings and evenings and most of what happened in between. Now he was pleased by the cool look of the little stream that ran beside the country road.

All of a sudden O'Malley stopped and stared. There beside the stream sat the most beautiful cat he had ever seen. She looked up at O'Malley, but she said not a word.

"I'm O'Malley," said the alley cat. "And what might your name be?"

The other cat lowered her blue eyes and curled her white tail around her feet and sighed a most unhappy sigh. "I'm Duchess," she told him.

O'Malley wondered what on earth she was sighing about. Duchess was a lovely name and she was a lovely cat. He quickly told her so.

She was not interested. "Please, Mr. O'Malley," she said. "I am in great trouble. Would you be so kind as to show me the way to Paris?"

"Show you the way?" O'Malley grinned his widest grin. "I won't show you the way," he said. "I'll take you there."

"You will?" said the beautiful white cat.

"Oooh!" squeaked a high little voice behind O'Malley. "That will be wonderful!"

O'Malley turned and saw a fluffy white kitten who looked very much like Duchess.

"This is Marie," said Duchess.

A tan kitten and a gray kitten scampered up.

"And here are Toulouse and Berlioz," Duchess announced. "These are my children."

O'Malley felt his whiskers wilt. It had not entered his head that the beautiful cat might have a family to look after. Still, he had promised to take her to Paris, and he would do it, kittens and all.

"Which way, Mr. O'Malley?" asked Duchess.

"Oh, you're not going to walk!" said O'Malley.

"We aren't?" said Duchess. "Then how shall we get there?"

"On a magic carpet," declared O'Malley. "You hide beside the road and you'll see."

So Duchess and her kittens hid. O'Malley climbed up into a tree and watched the road, and presently a magic carpet came into sight. It did not look a bit like a carpet. Actually, it was a truck, but O'Malley decided it would do. He leapt from his tree, landed on the hood of the truck, and yowled.

The driver screamed and the truck skidded and stopped. O'Malley jumped to the ground. "Quick!" he cried to Duchess. "Get in!" And before the driver could start his truck again, Duchess and her kittens were hidden in the back, along with O'Malley. A moment later they were jouncing merrily toward Paris. Most happily, the truck turned out to be a milk truck, so the cats had a good breakfast.

Nothing lasts forever. The driver soon discovered that five cats were lapping cream in the back of his truck. He stopped again and he screamed again. He also threw several heavy objects.

"What a horrible person!" exclaimed Duchess after the man had rattled away in his truck.

O'Malley was not upset. "Human beings can be like that," he told Duchess. "Some of them dig cats and some of them don't."

"My friend Madame is not like that," said Duchess.

"Madame loves us," put in little Marie. "She says we're her greatest treasures."

"She's human?" asked O'Malley.

"But of course," said Duchess.

O'Malley knew then what Duchess was. She was an aristocat. Aristocats lived in houses and slept on velvet cushions. They knew a great deal about behaving properly, but not much about getting along in the world. They depended on humans for that.

"I wish we were at home now with Madame and Edgar," Marie whimpered.

"Edgar is Madame's butler," Duchess told O'Malley. "He always takes good care of us."

"If Madame loves you so much, and Edgar takes such good care of you, how did you get lost way out here in the country?" asked O'Malley.

Duchess looked troubled. "I don't know," she admitted. "Last night we went to sleep in our basket outside Madame's bedroom. This morning we woke up next to that little river. It is bewildering."

"Maybe it isn't as bewildering as all that," said O'Malley. "Maybe Madame decided she'd had it with cats. Maybe she's going to go in for canaries or goldfish or something."

"Impossible!" Duchess was indignant. "Only yesterday Madame made her will. We are to be her heirs, and Edgar will be our guardian."

"And if anything were to happen to you?" asked the canny alley cat.

"Then Edgar would inherit Madame's money," said Duchess. "He has served Madame for many years."

"Aha!" said O'Malley. So the butler had a good reason for getting rid of the aristocats!

Just then a field mouse scampered across the road in front of the cat.

"Look, Mama!" cried Marie. "A mouse! Why doesn't he stop and talk with us?"

"He is a country mouse, my darling," said Duchess. "He does not know us as Monsieur Roquefort does."

"Monsieur Roquefort is the nicest mouse," said Berlioz. "He lives behind the wall in Madame's drawing room."

For once in his life, O'Malley was speechless. So these cats hobnobbed with a mouse! It was incredible. It was against nature.

O'Malley was all for stopping another truck so they could continue their journey in comfort, but Duchess wouldn't hear of it. "I think drivers do not wish passengers," she said. "We will walk."

Walk, they did. They walked all day, and by the time they reached Paris it was quite dark and the kittens were staggering with weariness.

"Madame's house is near the Bois," said Duchess.

O'Malley looked at the kittens. "That's still a long way," he said. "The kids will never make it. Look, I've got a little place near here. It's kind of a penthouse pad. Why not stay over tonight and go on home in the morning?"

Berlioz sat down on the pavement and went to sleep.

"I suppose that would be best," agreed Duchess. She nudged Berlioz awake, and the aristocats followed O'Malley down a side street, through a broken door, and up two flights of stairs. Then they were out on the rooftops which O'Malley loved. He led the way past crumbling chimneys until they came to a skylight that had very little glass left in it. A shrill blast of music blared out at them.

"Uh-oh!" said O'Malley. "That's Scat Cat."

"A friend of yours?" asked Duchess.

"The greatest," said O'Malley, but he didn't look happy. Usually nothing pleased him more than to have Scat Cat and his gang drop in. However, Duchess and her kittens were tired. They needed peace and quiet, not a jam session. And Scat Cat was an extremely tough character. What would aristocat Duchess think of him?

O'Malley need not have worried. Aristocat Duchess had beautiful manners. She said she would love to see O'Malley's penthouse pad and to meet his friends.

The pad was only a dusty attic, but Duchess didn't notice this. She said good evening to Scat Cat. He stopped tooting his battered brass horn and beamed at her. She greeted Scat Cat's friends—the cat who played the piano and the cat who plucked the bass violin and the cat who strummed the guitar. She told them she liked their mad music. They laughed, and they played louder and louder and faster and faster.

O'Malley watched and listened and enjoyed. And he thought warm thoughts about aristocats in general and Duchess in particular.

When Scat Cat and his group finished playing, they went out through the skylight, and the aristocats settled down to sleep in a sagging old bed in a corner of the attic. O'Malley slept very little. He was worried. What would happen when Duchess returned to Madame?

The next day O'Malley went with Duchess and the kittens to the elegant old house near the Bois. He had made up his mind; he wanted a good look at Edgar the butler.

O'Malley hid behind the gatepost and watched as Duchess and the kittens mewed at the door. The butler came out. It seemed to O'Malley that the man was overjoyed to see the aristocats. He uttered glad little cries and welcomed them in. Then the door closed on them.

So all was well. Or was it? O'Malley began to pace up and down. He had not paced long before a small, excited mouse scooted out through the gate.

"O'Malley?" shrieked the mouse.

O'Malley guessed that this must be Roquefort. "What's up?" asked the cat.

"Edgar did it!" cried the mouse. "He's the one who stole Duchess and the kittens. Now he's put them in a sack and he's called the express company. He's going to ship them to Timbuktu. Duchess told me to get O'Malley."

O'Malley's eyes gleamed with yellow fire. "You go find Scat Cat and his gang," he told the mouse.

"Scat Cat?" quavered poor little Roquefort.

"He's an alley cat," said O'Malley. "He lives on the Left Bank. Tell him O'Malley sent you and you won't have a bit of trouble."

Roquefort scampered off looking quite worried and O'Malley went in through the gate and around to the back door, where he hid. Soon the door opened and the butler came out. He was carrying a sack which wriggled and mewed. "Don't cry," the butler told the sack. "You're going on a nice long trip. Then I'll inherit Madame's money!"

O'Malley trailed the butler across the garden to the carriage house, where a pretty little mare was munching oats. The mare stared at O'Malley. Then she stared at Edgar, who hauled a trunk out of a corner and put the sack into it.

O'Malley felt he could not wait for Scat Cat. The time had come for action. He leapt at Edgar.

The butler shouted and fell, but he got up again and snatched a pitchfork. He chased O'Malley into a corner. Then he threw open the door that led from the carriage house out to the back lane.

O'Malley's heart leapt, for in the lane stood a small, excited mouse surrounded by a number of large, excited cats. The cats promptly swarmed into the carriage house and all over Edgar.

With the wicked Edgar beset by cats. O'Malley came out of his corner and got to work on the trunk. In seconds he had the lid up and was helping Duchess claw her way free of the sack.

The little mare reared and kicked at her stall, and the door crashed open.

Duchess and her kittens scrambled out of the trunk as Scat Cat yelled, "One side!" The alley cats then tumbled Edgar into the trunk.

BANG! Down came the lid of the trunk.

For the first time, the little mare spoke. "Let me!" she said. She turned her hindquarters toward the trunk and kicked. The trunk slid out through the open door of the carriage house and came to rest in the lane.

A few minutes later, the truck from the express company came chugging along. It stopped and two men climbed out and loaded the trunk into the truck. As they drove away, O'Malley chuckled. "I hope Edgar likes Timbuktu," he said.

The cats and the mouse and the mare paraded across the garden and mewed and squeaked and whinnied at the back door until Madame came down to let them in. Madame was so happy to see Duchess and the kittens that she cried. Then she invited Duchess's new friends in for a nice bowl of cream. O'Malley enjoyed it. He enjoyed it so much that he never again left the old house near the Bois, or Madame, or Duchess and the kittens.

As for Edgar, he never came back. This is not surprising. Timbuktu is a long way from Paris.

101 DALMATIANS

Lucky Puppy was a Dalmatian. This means, among other things, that he was a white dog with black spots. Lucky lived in London in a nice little house on a quiet little street. His father, Pongo, lived there, too. So did his mother, Perdita. And so did Lucky's fourteen brothers and sisters.

Lucky Puppy and his family were as happy as could be. They had the three most wonderful human beings in all of London, if not in all of the world. They had Roger. He was tall and thin. He smoked a pipe and played the piano and sang. They had Anita, Roger's wife. She laughed a lot and she dusted things—but not too often. And they had Nanny Cook. She was a dear, round, soft little lady who puttered and pattered and made delicious things for Roger and Anita to eat.

One day the doorbell rang in the nice little house on the quiet little street. Anita opened the door, and there stood Cruella de Vil.

"Oh, dear!" said Perdita. She hid under the sofa.

"Blast!" said Roger. He went upstairs to the attic and shut the door.

No one in that nice little house liked Cruella de Vil. She waved her skinny arms too much. She smoked cigarettes in a long holder and she scattered her ashes about. She called Anita "Darling," but she never sounded as if she meant it. Anita let her in only because they had been in school together.

"Darling!" cried Cruella. She swept in through the little hallway. "Where are they?"

"What?" said Anita.

"The puppies!" shrieked Cruella. She stormed into the parlor, where Lucky and his brothers and sisters were watching television. "I'll take them!"

The door to the attic opened and Roger put his head out. "You'll take what?" he demanded.

Cruella reached into her handbag and took out her checkbook. "How much do you want?" she asked.

"For Lucky?" gasped Anita. "And Spot and Dot and Freckles and...and...Oh, Cruella, we couldn't part with them."

"Don't be silly, Anita," snapped Cruella. "You can't possibly keep fifteen puppies."

Roger marched down the attic stairs. "We are not selling them," he said. "And that's final!"

"Why you horrid man!" shouted Cruella. She put her checkbook back in her handbag. "All right, but you'll be sorry. I'm through with all of you!"

With that, she rushed out and banged the door so hard that the glass broke.

Roger went out to buy new glass for the door, and everyone forgot about Cruella de Vil.

One sharp and frosty night a few weeks later, Roger and Anita went off for a brisk walk with Pongo and Perdita. Nanny Cook was in the kitchen, tucking Lucky Puppy and his brothers and sisters into their basket, when the doorbell rang. "Now who could that be?" wondered Nanny Cook. She went and opened the door, which was the best way to find out.

There on the doorstep were two men. One was tall and thin and homely. The other was short and fat and homely. They said they were from the electric company. However, they locked dear Nanny Cook in the attic, and men from the electric company would never do that. And once Nanny Cook was locked up, they put Lucky Puppy and all his brothers and sisters into a big satchel. Then they ran out to their truck, which was parked at the door, threw the satchel into the truck, and sped away.

The puppies were terribly frightened. They felt the truck swerve to the right and turn to the left. After a while, Lucky Puppy could not hear the street noises of London. He knew they must be in the country.

It seemed hours before the truck stopped and the puppies heard someone open a big, squeaking gate. The truck drove on for a short distance and stopped again. The puppies were lifted and carried, bump-bumping in the satchel. A door opened and closed, and footsteps echoed on a bare floor. At last the satchel was put down, and Lucky and his brothers and sisters were tumbled out, heads over tails.

Lucky shook himself and looked around. They were in a great room that smelled of dampness and mold and tired old furniture. There were broken chairs and teetering tables and a sofa with springs coming out of the bottom. And there were Dalmatian puppies.

Lucky blinked. He saw dozens of Dalmatian puppies. He saw scores of Dalmatian puppies. Lucky could not count very well but he thought there must have been nearly a hundred Dalmatian puppies in that dank and dusty old room.

In addition to the little Dalmatians, there were the two horrid men who had locked Nanny Cook in the attic. Lucky growled at the two men.

"Don't do that," warned one of the Dalmatians.

"Those are the Badun brothers. They're mean."

"The Badun brothers?" said Lucky.

The strange puppy nodded. "Horace and Jasper Badun. They work for Cruella de Vil."

At the mention of Cruella, Lucky gave a frightened little bark. So did his brothers and sisters.

"Quiet!" yelled one of the Baduns.

"They don't like it if we bark," whispered one of the strange puppies.

"May I ask who you are?" asked Lucky. "Where did you all come from?"

"We don't have names," answered one of the puppies. "We were bought from the pet shops, and no one ever gave us names."

"We weren't bought from a pet shop," said Lucky. "We were stolen!"

"You were?" said the other puppy. "I wonder why."

Lucky and his brothers and sisters wondered, too. If it had anything to do with Cruella de Vil, they were sure they weren't going to like it.

"It will be all right," said Lucky stoutly. "They'll be looking for us."

"Who will?" asked the strange puppy.

"Mother and Dad," said Lucky, "and Roger and Anita and Nanny Cook. I'll bet they're looking for us right now."

Lucky and his brothers and sisters made themselves as comfortable as they could, and they waited. The night passed and day came. The Baduns fed all the puppies canned dog food for breakfast. Then they watched television, which they liked a lot.

Day passed and the night came, and all the puppies had a supper of puppy biscuits and milk. Lucky munched his biscuit and listened. Somewhere outside a dog was barking. Lucky couldn't quite make out what he was saying.

After a while the barking stopped, and after another while Lucky felt a draft of cold air. Someone had opened a window in the old house; a breeze was blowing in through a small hole in the wall right behind the sofa.

"Rover?" said a voice from the wall. "Spotty?"

A lean, lank cat put his head in through the hole and looked at Lucky and the other puppies. "Good night!" said the cat. "There are a lot of you. I'm looking for fifteen spotted puppies who were stolen from London."

"My brothers and sisters and I were stolen," said Lucky Puppy.

"Fifteen of you?" said the cat. "But there must be almost a hundred puppies here."

"The others were bought and paid for," said Lucky. "The Baduns stole me and my brothers and sisters."

The cat saluted. "I'm Sergeant Tibs," he told Lucky. "The police are looking everywhere for you. We got word from London by the Twilight Bark."

Lucky knew about the Twilight Bark. In the evenings, dogs used a system of long and short barks to pass news along. Sometimes it was only gossip that went from dog to dog, but sometimes the Twilight Bark carried important information.

"Our colonel's a sheepdog," explained Sergeant Tibs. "He lives on the other side of the pasture. He got word from Old Towser up at Withermarsh that you were missing. Towser heard it from a barge dog who got it from the Great Dane near Tower Bridge. The Great Dane said something about Pongo."

"Good old Dad!" exclaimed Lucky Puppy.

"What about Dad?" yipped Rolly.

But the Baduns had heard them. "Hey!" yelled Horace. "What's that cat doing here?"

"I'll report to the Colonel," said Tibs, and he zipped out through the hole in the wall.

Lucky and his brothers and sisters crept into a corner, as far from the Baduns as they could get. "Dad's coming for us," said Lucky happily.

"Listen!" whispered Pepper.

Through the night, the puppies heard the deep, hoarse baying of a sheepdog.

"That must be the Colonel," said Lucky. "He's sending word to London." And Lucky Puppy curled up to sleep, feeling very lucky indeed.

When day came again the Baduns snapped on their television set so they could watch the early show while they opened the canned dog food. But before they could give the Dalmatians their breakfast, they heard the roar of a powerful car. Brakes screeched. A door slammed. Cruella de Vil rushed in, shouting and sprinkling her cigarette ashes in every direction.

"It's got to be done today!" cried Cruella.

Horace Badun looked at the Dalmatians. The Dalmatians retreated under chairs and behind tables.

"They aren't big enough," said Horace.

Sergeant Tibs the cat crept in through the hole in the wall.

"You couldn't get a dozen coats out of the whole caboodle," protested Jasper Badun.

"Coats?" said Sergeant Tibs.

"Coats?" echoed Lucky Puppy.

"She couldn't mean...dog-skin coats?" said Tibs.

"If I can't get a dozen coats, I'll get half a dozen," said Cruella. "The police are everywhere. I want the job done right away. I don't care how you do it, but do it!"

She slammed out. They heard her car roar away.

Horace sighed and picked up a poker.

"Put that down," said Jasper. He slumped on the sofa and stared at the television. "We can do it later. I want to watch this program."

So Horace put down the poker, and he, too, stared at the television.

"You kids better get out of here right now," whispered Sergeant Tibs. He shoved one of the nameless puppies toward the hole in the wall.

"It's too small," protested the pup.

"Squeeze!" ordered Tibs.

The pup squeezed, and he popped through.

"Shake a leg," urged Tibs.

Another pup squeezed through, and another, and another. Plaster crumbled and the hole got bigger.

"Step lively," whispered Tibs.

The Dalmatians stepped lively, pup after pup after pup. A small traffic jam occurred when plump little Rolly stuck fast in the hole, but Tibs braced himself and pushed hard, and Rolly scraped on through. Lucky slipped out after him, and Sergeant Tibs stepped through after Lucky.

"Now follow me," ordered Tibs to the multitude of Dalmatian puppies who waited in the hallway.

In the room behind them, there was a loud outcry. "They're gone!" yelled Jasper. "Quick! We'll run them down!"

Tibs and the Dalmatians raced up the staircase.

Jasper dashed out into the hall with the poker clenched in his fist. Horace followed, waving the broken leg of a chair.

"There they go!" shouted Horace.

Tibs and the puppies ran through an open door and hid under a bed. The puppies who couldn't get under the bed got under the bureau and behind the chairs.

Horace and Jasper came into the room, and Horace promptly looked under the bed.

Brave Sergeant Tibs leapt straight at Horace. The wicked Badun fell back, and the puppies scampered over him in a yipping black and white stream.

"Head them off!" yelled Horace.

But they swept around Jasper and down the stairs.

"In here, quick!" Tibs dodged under the staircase.

The puppies followed. They pressed themselves back against the wall and waited, hardly breathing.

Down the stairs thundered Horace and Jasper. Tibs and the puppies heard a door close. Then a second door closed, and a third. The Baduns were shutting off the Dalmatians' escape routes.

"Enough of this ring-around-the-rosy," muttered Jasper. The floor squeaked next to the stairs. "Here they are!" shouted Jasper. "We've got them!"

There was no place to hide as Jasper came on, a step at a time, his poker held high. Horace beat at the air with the chair leg. Lucky Puppy closed his eyes. He thought of his mother and father. He thought of Roger and Anita and Nanny Cook. A tear ran down his nose.

Then there was a fearful crash.

Lucky opened his eyes. There stood Pongo, his father, with his teeth bared.

Perdita, his gentle mother, jumped in through a shattered window. She growled and snapped at Horace.

"Give them what for!" yelled Jasper.

"I'll knock the spots off of you!" threatened Horace.

But Jasper never gave anyone what for, and Horace never knocked the spots off anyone. Pongo and Perdita fought like six dogs. They fought as dogs can fight only when their puppies are in danger. They leapt and growled and snarled and bit. Sergeant Tibs darted out from under the stairs.

"Blast them, Tibs!" bellowed an old sheepdog who had put his head in the window.

"No, no, Colonel!" said Tibs. "Retreat!"

"Oh, very well," huffed the sheepdog. "Retreat then. Retreat on the double!"

Sergeant Tibs led the retreat. He leapt out of the window. Behind him came Lucky and all of his brothers and sisters, and behind them came those scores of nameless puppies.

Perdita pulled Horace's coat sleeve out. Then she jumped through the window.

Pongo knocked Jasper into the fireplace. Then he jumped through the window.

"This way," barked the Colonel. A fresh snow had fallen during the night. The Dalmatians left hundreds of puppy tracks as they fled, but there

was no time to worry about this. They said a hasty good-bye to Colonel, that good old sheepdog. They thanked Sergeant Tibs, that noble cat. Then they were running toward London. Pongo and Perdita were in the front. Behind them ran Lucky and his brothers and sisters. Behind them came all those scores of Dalmatian pups. For Perdita had decided that not one little one would be left behind.

Along the way, dogs waited to help Pongo and Perdita and the puppies. At a farm a few miles from Cruella de Vil's house, a collie brought them some scraps to eat. Farther on, an old hound sheltered them in a barn. And in a village halfway to London, a sleek black Labrador met them with good news. There was a van leaving the village. It was bound for London, and there would be plenty of room in the back for the Dalmatians.

Pongo was happy to hear it. The puppies were tired and it was very cold. They were about to get up into the van when they heard a car on the road behind them.

"Pongo!" cried Perdita. "That's Cruella!"

And it was Cruella. She was driving her fancy car slowly, following the tracks the Dalmatians had left in the snow.

"Quick! In here!" said the Labrador.

The Dalmatians followed him. They crowded into an abandoned shop and hid. Cruella drove slowly, slowly down the street. When she reached the far end of the street, she turned and drove back.

"Oh, Pongo," said Perdita, "how will we get to the van?"

It was Lucky Puppy who found the way. He did it by accident. He fell into the fireplace. There was no fire, of course, but there was a great deal of soot. Lucky came out black from head to toe.

"That's it!" said Pongo. "Cruella is looking for Dalmatians. We'll be Labradors." He ran into the fireplace and rolled in the soot until he was black, too. He looked very much like a Labrador.

After that, all of the puppies rolled in the soot. So did Perdita. When they were ready, the dogs marched calmly out of the shop. They passed Cruella's car and walked up to the van that was ready to leave for London.

One after another, the puppies were lifted into the van. Lucky was in, and Patch and Dot and Blot and Pepper and most of the nameless ones. At last only one puppy remained on the street. As Pongo bent to pick him up, a tiny avalanche of snow came down from a roof and buried him.

Pongo snatched the pup up and put him into the van, but the dog was not quick enough. The snow had washed away the soot. Cruella, watching from her car, saw white fur and black spots.

"There they are!" shouted Cruella.

Pongo leapt in and the van began to move.

Cruella's car roared. Snow spun from the wheels.

Faster and faster went the van. But Cruella drew closer and closer. The dogs could see her face. She was screaming in anger. Then she began to scream in fear. There was a narrow bridge on the road ahead. There was room only for the van to pass. Cruella tried to stop, and her car spun sideways on the snow and slid into a ditch. The last the Dalmatians saw of her, she was standing beside the

wrecked car having a very nasty temper tantrum.

Pongo laughed and the puppies cheered. And when the van reached London, the Dalmatians jumped out and ran straight to that nice little house on that quiet little street.

Nanny Cook opened the door and the dogs streamed in. Nanny Cook was so excited, she didn't know what to do.

Anita was also excited, but she knew what to do. She began to dust the soot off the Dalmatians.

Roger knew what to do. He counted the Dalmatians. Pongo and Perdita were two. Their fifteen puppies made seventeen. And there were eighty-four other puppies besides. They had one hundred and one Dalmatians.

"I think we'd better get a bigger house," said Roger. "One in the country, perhaps. We could call it our Dalmatian plantation."

Roger did exactly that. And Pongo and Perdita and all the spotted puppies lived there happily ever after.

As for Cruella de Vil, she may still be screaming by the side of the road. No one knows, for no one ever went back to find out.

PINOCCHIO

One night, long, long ago, the Evening Star shone down across the dark sky. Its beams formed a shimmering pathway to a tiny village, and painted its humble roofs with stardust.

But the silent little town was deep in sleep. The only witness to the beauty of the night was a weary wayfarer who chanced to be passing through.

His clothes were gray with dust. His well-worn shoes pinched his feet; his back ached from the weight of the carpetbag slung over his shabby shoulder. To be sure, it was only a small carpetbag; but this wayfarer had a very small shoulder. As a matter of fact, he was an exceedingly small wayfarer. His name was Cricket, Jiminy Cricket.

He marveled at the radiant star; it seemed almost close enough to touch, and pretty as a picture. But at this moment Jiminy Cricket was not interested in pretty pictures. He was looking for a place to rest.

Suddenly he noticed a light in a window, and smoke curling from a chimney.

"Where there's smoke, there's a fire," he reasoned. "Where there's a fire, there's a hearth. And where there's a hearth, there *should* be a cricket!"

And with that, he hopped up to the windowsill and peered in. The room had a friendly look. So Jiminy crawled under the door, scurried over to the hearth, backed up against the glowing fireplace, and warmed his little britches.

It was no ordinary village home into which the

small wayfarer had stumbled. It was a workshop: the workshop of Geppetto the wood-carver. Old Geppetto was working late that night. He was making a puppet.

Geppetto lived alone except for his black kitten, Figaro, and a pet goldfish he called Cleo. But he had many friends; everyone knew and loved the kindly, white-haired old man. He had spent his whole life creating happiness for others.

It was the children who loved Geppetto best. He doctored their dolls, put clean sawdust into limp rag bodies, and painted fresh smiles on faded china faces. He fashioned new arms and legs for battered tin soldiers—and there was magic in his hands when he carved a toy.

Now, the weary old fellow put his tools away and surveyed his newest handiwork. The puppet he had made had the figure of a small boy. He was the right size for a small boy. He had the cute, round face of a small boy—except for one feature. The nose!

Geppetto had given him a very long and pointed nose, such a nose as no real boy ever possessed. A funny nose.

The old wood-carver stroked his chin and chuckled. "Woodenhead," he said, "you are finished, and you deserve a name. What shall I call you? I know—*Pinocchio!* Do you like it?" He worked the puppet's strings so that it nodded "Yes."

"That settles it!" cried Geppetto happily. "Pinocchio you are! And now," he yawned, "time for bed. Good night, Figaro! Good night, Cleo! Good night, Pinocchio!"

Jiminy Cricket was glad to hear these words, for he felt very sleepy. Geppetto put on a long white nightshirt and climbed creakily into bed, but he still sat admiring the puppet with its wooden smile.

"Look at him, Figaro!" he exclaimed. "He seems almost real. Wouldn't it be nice if he were alive?"

But the only answer from the kitten was a snore.

Long after Geppetto had gone to sleep, Jiminy

Cricket lay awake thinking. It made him sad to realize the old man's wish could never come true.

Suddenly he heard something. Music—mysterious music! He sat up and looked around the room. Then he saw a strange light—a brilliant glow, which grew more dazzling every minute. It was a star—the Evening Star, floating down from the sky and entering Geppetto's window!

Then in the center of the blinding glow appeared a beautiful lady dressed in robes of flowing blue.

"As I live and breathe!" Jiminy whispered in astonishment. "A fairy!"

The Blue Fairy bent over the old wood-carver and spoke to him ever so softly, so as not to disturb his slumber.

"Good Geppetto," she said, "you have given so much happiness to others, you deserve to have your wish come true!"

Then she turned to the wooden puppet. Holding out her glittering wand, she spoke these words:

"Little puppet made of pine,
Wake! The gift of life is thine!"

And when the wand touched him, Pinocchio came to life! First he blinked his eyes, then he raised his wooden arm and wiggled his jointed fingers.

"I can move!" he cried. "I can *talk!*"

"Yes, Pinocchio," the Blue Fairy smiled. "Geppetto needs a little son. So tonight I give you life."

"Then I'm a real boy!" cried Pinocchio joyfully.

"No," said the Fairy sadly. "There is no magic that can make us real. I have given you life—the rest is up to you."

"Tell me what I must do," begged Pinocchio. "I want to be a real boy!"

"Prove yourself brave, truthful, and unselfish," said the Blue Fairy. "Be a good son to Geppetto—make him proud of you! Then, someday, you will wake up and find yourself a real boy!"

"Whew! That won't be easy," thought Jiminy Cricket.

But the Blue Fairy also realized what a hard task she was giving Pinocchio. "The world is full of temptations," she continued. "You must learn to choose between right and wrong—"

"Right? Wrong?" questioned Pinocchio. "How will I know?"

Jiminy wrung his hands in desperation. But the wise Fairy was not yet finished. "Your conscience will tell you the difference between right and wrong," she explained.

"Conscience?" Pinocchio repeated. "What are conscience?"

That was too much for Jiminy Cricket. He hopped down where he could be seen.

"A conscience," he shouted, "is that still, small voice people won't listen to! That's the trouble with the world today!"

"Are *you* my conscience?" asked Pinocchio eagerly.

Jiminy was embarrassed, but the Blue Fairy came to his rescue. "Would you like to be Pinocchio's conscience?" she said with a smile. "You seem a man of the world. What is your name?"

Jiminy was flattered. "Jiminy Cricket," he answered.

"Kneel, Mister Cricket," commanded the Blue Fairy.

Jiminy knelt and trembled as her wand touched him.

"I dub you Pinocchio's conscience," she proclaimed, "Lord High Keeper of the Knowledge of Right and Wrong! Arise—*Sir* Jiminy Cricket!"

And when the dusty little cricket rose, his shabby old clothes were gone and he was clad in elegant raiment from head to foot.

"Don't I get a badge or something?" he asked.

"We'll see," the Blue Fairy said with a smile.

"Make it a gold one?" urged Jiminy.

"Perhaps, if you do your job well," she said. "I

leave Pinocchio in your hands. Give him the benefit of your advice and experience. Help him to be a real boy!"

It was a serious moment for the little cricket. He promised to help Pinocchio as much as he could, and to stick by him through thick and thin. The Blue Fairy thanked him.

"And now, Pinocchio," she said, "be a good boy—and always let your conscience be your guide! Don't be discouraged because you are different from the other boys! Remember—*any child who is not good, might just as well be made of wood!*" The Blue Fairy backed slowly away. There was one last soft chord of music and she was gone.

Pinocchio and Jiminy stared silently at the spot where the Fairy had stood, half hoping she might return. The little cricket finally broke the spell.

"Say, she's all right, son!" he exclaimed. "Remember what she told you—always let your conscience be your guide!"

"Yes, sir, I will!" answered Pinocchio.

"And when you need me, whistle," said Jiminy, "like this!"

"Like this?" Pinocchio tried but no sound came.

So Jiminy sang him a little lecture-lesson, which went something like this:

> "*When you get in trouble*
> *And you don't know right from wrong,*
> *Give a little whistle,*
> *Give a little whistle.*
> *When you meet temptation*
> *And the urge is very strong,*
> *Give a little whistle,*
> *Give a little whistle.*"

Then he began dancing down the strings of a violin on the bench, balancing himself with his small umbrella.

"Take the straight and narrow path
And if you start to slide,
Give a little whistle,
Give a little whistle—"

Just then the violin string broke. Jiminy fell over backward, but picked himself up and finished, "and always let your conscience be your guide!"

Pinocchio watched entranced as the little cricket went on dancing. Finally he too jumped up and tried to make his wooden feet go through the same steps. But he danced too close to the edge of the workbench, lost his balance, and fell clatteringly to the floor.

The noise woke Geppetto. "Who's there?" he called.

Pinocchio, on the floor, answered, "It's *me!*"

Geppetto's teeth chattered with fright. "Figaro, there's somebody in here!" he whispered. "A burglar, maybe! Come, we'll catch him!"

Then to his surprise, he noticed his puppet, which he had left on the workbench, lying on the floor.

"Why, Pinocchio!" he exclaimed. "How did you get down there?" He picked the puppet up and set him back on the bench. Imagine his surprise when Pinocchio answered!

"I fell down!" he said.

Geppetto stared. "What! You're talking?" he cried. "No! You're only a marionette. You can't talk!"

"Yes, I can," insisted the puppet. "I can move, too!"

The old man backed away. "No, no" he argued. "I must be dreaming! I will pour water on myself! I will stick myself with pins!"

Geppetto made sure he was awake. "Now we will see who is dreaming," he challenged. "Go on—say something!"

Pinocchio laughed merrily. "Do it again!" he begged. "You're awful funny! I like you!"

"You *do* talk," said the old man in a hushed voice. "Pinocchio! It's a miracle! Figaro! Cleo! Look—he's alive!"

Geppetto didn't know whether to laugh or cry, he was so happy. "This calls for a celebration!" he announced. He turned on a music box and began to dance. He went to his toy shelves and filled his arms with playthings. It was just like Christmas for Pinocchio. He couldn't decide which toy to play with first!

But the music box ran down and the celebration ended.

"Now it is time for bed," said the old wood-carver. "Come, Pinocchio. You shall sleep here in this dresser drawer." He tucked Pinocchio in and said, "Sleep tight, Pinocchio!"

That night Jiminy Cricket did an unusual thing—for him. He prayed. He prayed that Pinocchio might never disappoint that kind, happy old man or the lovely Blue Fairy, and that he himself might be a good conscience, so Pinocchio would soon earn the right to be a real boy.

All was still in the little shop. High in the sky the Evening Star twinkled softly, as though smiling approval of a good night's work.

Morning dawned bright and clear. As the school bells rang out over the village, their clamor sent pigeons flying from the old belfry like colored fans spread against the white clouds.

The school bells carried a special message of joy to old Geppetto. Today his own son was to join the other little ones on their way to school!

Pinocchio too was impatient. His face, shiny from scrubbing, beamed with excitement. Even Figaro and Cleo realized it was a gala day.

At last Pinocchio was pronounced ready. Geppetto opened the door. For the first time the puppet looked out at the wide, wide world. How beautiful it was!

"What are those?" he asked, pointing down the street.

"Those are the children, bless them!" Geppetto answered. "They are the boys and girls—your schoolmates, Pinocchio!"

"Real boys?" Pinocchio asked eagerly.

"Yes, my son. And if you study hard, you'll soon be as smart as they are. Wait a minute—your books!"

Little Figaro appeared at the door, tugging the strap which held Pinocchio's schoolbooks.

"Ah, thank you, Figaro. You too want to help! Pinocchio, here are your books. Remember, be a good boy. Choose your friends carefully; shun evil companions. Mind the teacher—"

"Good-bye!" shouted Pinocchio, pulling carelessly away. But he thought better of it, ran back, and threw his arms around Geppetto. "Good-bye, Father," he said shyly; then off he marched, his books under his arm, chock-full of good resolutions.

Jiminy Cricket heard the school bell and jumped up in a great hurry. Suppose Pinocchio had gone off to school without him! If ever a small boy needs a conscience, it is on his first day at school. A fine time to oversleep, Jiminy thought. Then he stuffed his shirt hastily inside his trousers, grabbed his hat, and rushed out.

"Hey, Pinoke!" he called. "Wait for me!"

After Geppetto saw Pinocchio safely off to school, he went cheerily to his workbench.

"An extra mouth to feed, Figaro," he chuckled to the kitten. "Yet what a joy it is to have someone to work for!"

But alas, many a dreary day and night were to pass before the old wood-carver saw his boy again! For in spite of Geppetto's warning, Pinocchio fell into bad company. He met two scheming adventurers—a fox and a cat, the worst pair of scoundrels in the whole countryside.

Run down at the heel and patched at the seat, these villains managed somehow to look like elegant gentlemen out for a stroll. But as usual, they were up to no good.

Suddenly, "Look!" cried the sharp-eyed fox, who went by the name of J. Worthington Foulfellow, alias Honest John. "Do you see what I see?" He pointed with his cane. The stupid cat, who was called Gideon, stared at Pinocchio.

"A puppet that walks!" marveled Foulfellow. "A live puppet—a marionette without strings! A breathing woodenhead!"

And before Pinocchio knew what had happened, he was lying flat on his face. Something had tripped

him up, and that something was a cane, thrust between his feet by the sly old fox.

"My dear young man! I'm so sorry," Foulfellow apologized, helping Pinocchio to his feet. "A most regrettable accident—Mr.—er—"

"Pinocchio," answered the puppet cheerfully.

"Ha, ha, Pinocchio," began Foulfellow, "you were going a little too fast! A little too fast, and in the *wrong* directon. Now I have a plan for you. Come..."

"But I'm on my way to school," said Pinocchio.

"To school? Nonsense!" said Foulfellow. "I have a much better plan.

"You're too bright a boy to waste your time in school," said Foulfellow. "Isn't he, Gideon?" Gideon nodded.

"You deserve a trip to Pleasure Island, my boy," said sly old Foulfellow.

"Pleasure Island?" repeated Pinocchio.

"Pleasure Island!" cried Foulfellow. "Where every day is a holiday, with fireworks, brass bands, parades—a paradise for boys! Why, I can see you now—lolling under a doughnut tree, a lollipop in each hand, gazing off at the pink Ice-Cream Mountains—think of it, Pinocchio!"

It was a tempting picture the sly fox painted. "Well, I *was* going to school," said Pinocchio. He hesitated. "But perhaps I could go to Pleasure Island first—for a little while..."

Jiminy Cricket came panting along just in time to see the three of them stroll off arm in arm.

"Oh, what a woodenhead he is!" thought Jiminy Cricket. But he followed loyally.

Soon they came to a great coach, piled to the brim with boys—eager, noisy, impudent boys! Laughing and shouting, Pinocchio climbed aboard.

"Good-bye!" Pinocchio called to the fox. "I'll never be able to thank you for this!"

"Think nothing of it, my boy," said the fox. "Seeing you happy is our only reward. Our only reward—reward—*reward!*" he kept repeating until the wicked-looking Coachman slipped him a large sack of gold. The fox had sold Pinocchio for gold!

Jiminy Cricket saw the Coachman crack his long blacksnake whip, and the coach start to move. The coach was drawn by twelve sorrowful-looking little donkeys, who seemed to feel very bad. "Tsk! Tsk! Tsk!" they said, every time the Coachman's whip descended. But nobody could hear them because of the boys' shouting.

"Three cheers for anything," they yelled, throwing their caps into the air as the coach rolled away. "Hurray for Pleasure Island!"

Jiminy made a last desperate effort. He hopped onto the rear axle of the coach and rode along. Certain that Pinocchio was headed for disaster, the loyal little cricket went with him just the same.

The journey was an unhappy one for Jiminy. At the waterfront, the passengers boarded a ferryboat for Pleasure Island, and the little cricket suffered from seasickness during the entire voyage.

But physical discomfort was not what bothered him most. He was worried about Pinocchio, who promptly made friends with the worst boy in the crowd—a no-good named "Lampwick." Lampwick talked out of the corner of his mouth, and was very untidy. Yet Pinocchio cherished his friendship.

Jiminy tried to warn Pinocchio, but the heedless puppet refused to listen. Finally the ferry docked and the boys swarmed down the gangplank onto Pleasure Island.

Bands played loudly; wonderful circuses performed along the streets, which were paved with cookies and lined with doughnut trees. Lollipops and cupcakes grew on bushes, and fountains spouted lemonade and soda pop. The Mayor of Pleasure Island made a speech of welcome and urged the boys to enjoy themselves.

Yes, Pleasure Island seemed to be all the fox had claimed for it, and more. Only Jiminy Cricket was skeptical. He felt that there was more to all this than appeared on the surface. But weeks went by, and seldom did Jiminy get close enough to Pinocchio to warn him. He was always in the midst of the fun, and his friend Lampwick was the ringleader of the horde of carefree, mischievous boys.

They smashed windows and burned schoolbooks; in fact they did whatever they felt like doing, no matter how destructive. They ate until they nearly burst. And always the Coachman and Mayor encouraged them to "Have a good time—while you can!"

And all the while the poor little donkeys—who performed all the hard labor on the island—looked very sad and said, "Tsk! Tsk! Tsk!"

One day Pinocchio and Lampwick were lazily floating in a canoe along the Lemonade River, which flowed between the Ice-Cream Mountains. Chocolate cattails grew thickly along the banks, lollipop trees drooped overhead, and the canoe was piled high with sweets.

"This is too good to be true, Lampwick," Pinocchio sighed blissfully. "I could stay here forever!"

"Aw, this is kid stuff," retorted Lampwick. "Let's go where we can have some real fun!"

"Where?" asked Pinocchio curiously.

"I'll show you," said Lampwick. So they pulled the canoe up on the bank, and Lampwick led the way to Tobacco Lane.

Here the fences were made of cigars, cigarettes and matches grew on bushes, and there were rows of cornstalks with corncob pipes on them. Lampwick lit a cigar and began smoking.

Pinocchio hesitated. Finally he picked a corncob

pipe and began to puff timidly.

"Aw, you smoke like my granmudder," jeered Lampwick. "Take a big drag, Pinoke—like dis!"

Under Lampwick's instruction, Pinocchio soon found himself smoking like a chimney. Just then, along came Jiminy. How sad the little cricket felt when he saw this you will never know. While he had known for a long time that Pinocchio had fallen into evil ways, Jiminy did not realize he had sunk to such depths.

Well, he had tried everything—except force. Would that make the lad come to his senses? He decided to try. He shook his little fist angrily. "So it's come to this, has it?" he shouted. "SMOKING!"

Pinocchio gave him a careless glance. "Yeah," he answered out of the corner of his mouth, in imitation of Lampwick. "So what?"

"Just this!" Jiminy exploded. "You're making a disgusting spectacle of yourself. You're going home this minute!"

Lampwick, who had never seen Jiminy before, was curious. "Who's de insect, Pinoke?" he asked.

"Jiminy? Why, he's my conscience," explained Pinocchio.

Lampwick began to laugh. "You mean you take advice from a *beetle*?" he remarked insultingly. "Say, I can't waste time wid a sap like you. So long!" And he strolled away.

"Lampwick! Don't go!" cried Pinocchio. "Now see what you've done, Jiminy! Lampwick was my best friend!"

That was too much for the little cricket. "So *he's* your best friend," he said angrily. "Well, Pinocchio, that's the last straw. I'm through! I'm taking the next boat out of here!"

Pinocchio hesitated but temptation was too strong. He couldn't give Lampwick up. He started off after him, full of apologies.

"Hey wait, Lampwick!" he called. "I'm coming with *you*!"

That was the end as far as Jiminy was concerned. "So he prefers to remain with that hoodlum, and allow him to insult *me*, his conscience?" he muttered. "Well, from now on he can paddle his own canoe. I'm going home!"

And he started toward the entrance gate, so upset that he did not notice how dark and forlorn Pleasure Island looked. There wasn't a boy in sight on the wide streets.

Jiminy's only thought was to get away quickly. He was just about to pound angrily on the gate when he heard voices on the other side. He tried to listen, and became conscious of a reddish glow which cast great, frightening shadows against the high stone walls. The shadows looked like prison guards, and they carried guns!

Jiminy jumped up and peered fearfully through the keyhole. In the cove, lit by flaming torches, he saw something that made his blood turn cold.

The ferryboat stood waiting, stripped of its decorations. The dock swarmed with howling, braying donkeys—fat ones and thin ones, many of whom still wore boys' hats and shoes. Huge, apelike guards herded them into crates, assisted by the Coachman, who cracked his whip brutally over the poor donkeys' heads.

The little cricket shuddered. At last he understood the meaning of Pleasure Island. This, then, was what became of lazy, good-for-nothing boys! They made donkeys of themselves! This was Pinocchio's fate, unless—

Forgetting his anger, Jiminy leapt to the ground and started back toward Tobacco Lane. He must warn Pinocchio to leave at once.

"Pinocchio!" he yelled. "Pinocchio!" But his cries only echoed through the empty streets.

Not far away, Pinocchio was still looking for Lampwick. He wandered unhappily past pie trees and popcorn shrubs. The island suddenly seemed strange, deserted.

Then he heard a frightened voice say, "Here I am!"

"Lampwick!" Pinocchio answered joyfully. "Where are you?"

Just then a little donkey emerged from some bushes. "Ssh!" he whispered. "Stop yelling! They'll hear us!"

Pinocchio stared. The donkey spoke in Lampwick's voice!

"This is no time for jokes," Pinocchio said crossly. "What are you doing in that donkey suit?"

"This ain't no donkey suit, Pinoke," the frightened voice replied, "I *am* a donkey!"

Pinocchio laughed. "You a donkey?" For he still thought it was a joke. "Ha ha ha! *He-Haw! He-Haw! He-Haw!*"

Pinocchio turned pale, but he couldn't stop. He was braying like a donkey! He put his hand over his mouth.

The little donkey came closer to him. "That's the first sign of donkey fever," he whispered. "That's how I started."

"Then—you *are* Lampwick! What happened?"

"Donkey fever," replied Lampwick, "and you've got it, too!"

Pinocchio's head began to buzz like a hive of bees. He reached up and felt something horrible. Two long, hairy ears were growing out of his head!

"You've got it all right!" whispered Lampwick. "Look behind you!"

Pinocchio looked and discovered that he had a long tail. He began to tremble, and was no longer able to stand up straight. Then he found himself on all fours, like a donkey!

"Help! Help!" he shrieked. "Jiminy! Jiminy Cricket!"

Jiminy Cricket ran toward them, but he saw that he was too late.

"Oh! Oh! Oh me, oh my!" he groaned. "Look at you! Come on! Let's get away from here before you're a complete donkey!"

This time nobody argued with the little cricket. As he fled toward the high stone wall, Pinocchio and the donkey that had once been Lampwick followed as fast as their legs would carry them. But as they rounded a corner, they came face-to-face with the Coachman and his armed guards. They turned and dashed toward the opposite wall.

"There they go! That's the two that's missing!" yelled the Coachman. "After them! Sound the alarm!"

Instantly the air was filled with the sound of sirens and the baying of bloodhounds. Searchlights began to play over the island, and bullets whizzed past the ears of the escaping prisoners. They expected to be shot at any minute.

Pinocchio and Jiminy reached the wall and managed to climb to the top before the apelike guards got within shooting distance. But Pinocchio looked down and saw a little donkey choking and kicking as he was caught with a rope lasso. It was Lampwick.

"Go on, Pinoke!" he cried. "It's all over wit me!"

A lump came in Pinocchio's throat. After all, Lampwick was his friend. But there was nothing he could do. He turned his back and said a silent prayer. Then he and Jiminy dived into the sea.

Bullets splashed all around them in the water, but by some miracle neither of them was hit. Finally a thick fog hid them from the glaring searchlights, and the sound of the guns died away. They had escaped!

It was a long, hard swim back to the mainland. When they reached shore, Pinocchio longed to see the cozy little cottages and his dear, kind father once more. Pleasure Island, and all it stood for, now seemed like a bad dream. But they were by no means at the end of their journey, for home was still many weary miles away.

It was winter when at last one evening they limped into the village. They hurried through the drifting snow to Geppetto's shop. Pinocchio pounded on the door with eager fists.

"Father! Father!" he cried. "It's me! It's Pinocchio!"

But the only reply was the howling of the wintry wind.

"He must be asleep," said Pinocchio, and he knocked again. But again there was no answer.

Worried, Pinocchio hastened to the window and peered in. The house was empty! Everything was shrouded and dusty.

"He's gone, Jiminy," said Pinocchio sorrowfully. "My father's gone away!"

"Looks like he's gone for good, too," said Jiminy. "What'll we do?"

"I don't know." Pinocchio sat down on the doorstep shivering. A tear came from his eye, ran down his long nose, and froze into a tiny, sparkling icicle. But Pinocchio didn't even bother to wipe it off. He felt terrible.

Just then a gust of wind blew around the corner, carrying a piece of paper. Jiminy hopped over to see what it was.

"Hey, Pinoke, it's a letter!" he exclaimed.

"Oh! Maybe it's from my father!" cried Pinocchio, and he quickly took the note from Jiminy and tried to read it. But alas, the marks on the paper meant nothing to him.

"You see, if you had gone to school you could read your father's letter," Jiminy reminded him. "Here—give it to me!"

The little cricket began to read the note aloud, and this is what it said:

"Dear Pinocchio:

"I heard you had gone to Pleasure Island, so I got a small boat and started off to search for you. Everyone said it was a dangerous voyage, but Figaro, Cleo, and I thought we could reach you and save you from a terrible fate.

"We weathered the storms, and finally reached the Terrible Straits. But just as we came in sight of our goal, out of the sea rose Monstro, the Terror of the Deep—the giant whale who swallows ships whole. He opened his jaws. In we went—boat and all..."

Here Pinocchio's sobs interrupted Jiminy's reading of the letter as he realized Geppetto's plight.

"Oh, my poor, poor father!" the puppet moaned. "He's dead! And it's all my fault!" He began to weep bitterly.

"But he isn't dead!" said Jiminy, and read on.

"So now, dear son, we are living at the bottom of the ocean in the belly of the whale. But there is very little to eat here, and we cannot exist much longer. So I fear you will never again see

Your loving father,
GEPPETTO."

"Hurrah! Hurrah!" shouted Pinocchio.

"Hurrah for what!" asked Jiminy somewhat crossly. It did not seem to him to be quite the time for cheers.

"Don't you see, Jiminy?" cried Pinocchio. "My father is still alive! There may be time to save him!"

"Save him?" said Jiminy stupidly. Then suddenly

a light dawned. "You don't mean *you*—"

"Yes!" announced Pinocchio. "I'm going after him. It's my fault he's down there in the whale; I'm going to the bottom of the ocean and rescue him!"

"But Pinocchio, you might be killed!" warned the cricket.

"I don't mind," declared Pinocchio. "What does life mean to me without my father? I've got to save him!"

Jiminy stared with open mouth. He hardly recognized this new Pinocchio—a brave, unselfish Pinocchio who stood there in place of the weak, foolish puppet he had known before.

"But think how far it is to the seashore—" he began.

Pinocchio looked thoughtful, but not for long. "I don't care. No place is too far for me to go after my father."

Just then, with a flutter of wings, a beautiful white dove settled gracefully down in the snow beside them.

"I will take you to the seashore," she said softly.

"You?" Pinocchio stared. But he did not see the tiny gold crown on the dove's head. It was she who had dropped the letter from the sky. She was his own dear Blue Fairy, disguised as a dove.

"Yes, I will help you," she assured him.

"How could a little dove carry me to the seashore?"

"Like this!"

And the dove began to grow and grow, until she was larger than an eagle. "Jump on my back," she commanded. Pinocchio obeyed.

"Good-bye, Jiminy Cricket," he said. "I may never see you again." He waved his hand to his little friend. "Thank you for all you've done!"

"Good-bye, nothing!" retorted Jiminy, and he too jumped on the back of the great white dove. "You're not leaving me! We'll see this through together!"

The dove raised her wide wings and rose from the ground. Higher and higher they flew, till the village disappeared and all they could see beneath them was whirling snow.

All night they flew through the storm. When morning came, the sun shone brightly. The dove's wings slowed down and she glided to earth at the edge of a cliff. Far below, the sea lay churning and lashing like a restless giant.

"I can take you no farther," said the dove. "Are you quite sure you want to go on this dangerous mission?"

"Yes," said Pinocchio. "Thank you for the ride. Good-bye!"

"Good-bye, Pinocchio," the dove replied. "Good luck!"

And she grew small again and flew away. Neither Pinocchio nor Jiminy realized that she was the Blue Fairy, but they were very grateful.

As soon as the dove was out of sight, Pinocchio tied a big stone to his donkey tail, to anchor him to the floor of the ocean. Then he smiled bravely at Jiminy, who smiled back, and together they leapt off the cliff.

The weight of the stone caused Pinocchio to sink at once. By clinging desperately to him, little Jiminy managed to stay close by. They landed, picked themselves up, and peered about. They were at the very bottom of the sea.

At first it seemed dark; they were many fathoms deep. Gradually Pinocchio's eyes became accustomed to the greenish light which filtered down into the submarine forest.

Giant clumps of seaweed waved overhead, like the branches of trees. Among them darted lovely bright objects, like birds or living flowers. They soon saw that these brilliant creatures were fish of all descriptions.

However, Pinocchio was in no frame of mind to make a study of the citizens of the sea. He walked along, peering into every cave and grotto in search of the great whale. But the stone attached to his tail made him move slowly, and he grew impatient.

"I wish we knew just where to look," he thought. "Jiminy, where do you suppose Monstro might be?"

"Don't know, I'm sure," replied Jiminy. "But we might ask some of these—er, people. I'll inquire here."

He knocked politely on an oyster. Its shell opened.

"Pardon me, Pearl," Jiminy began, "but could you tell me where we might find Monstro the Whale?"

To his surprise, the shell closed with a sharp click and the oyster scuttled off into a kelp bush as though frightened.

"Hm! That's funny!" remarked Jiminy.

Just then a school of tropical fish approached, brightly beautiful and extremely curious.

"I wonder," Pinocchio began, "if you could tell me where to find Monstro—"

But the lovely little creatures darted away before he had finished speaking. It was as though

Pinocchio had threatened to harm them in some way.

A bit farther along, they encountered a herd of tiny sea horses, grazing on the sandy bottom. Pinocchio tried once more.

"Could you tell me," he asked, "where I might find Monstro the Whale?"

But the sea horses fled, their little ears raised in alarm.

"You know what I think?" exclaimed Jiminy. "I think everybody down here is afraid of Monstro! Why, they run away at the very mention of his name! He must be awful. Do you think we should go on?"

"Certainly!" declared Pinocchio. "I'm not afraid!"

So they went on. It was a strange journey. Sometimes the water grew very dark, and tiny phosphorescent fish glowed like fireflies in the depths. They learned to be careful not to step on the huge flowers which lay on the ocean's floor. For they were not flowers but sea anemones, which could reach up and capture whatever came within their grasp.

Striped fish glared at them from seaweed thickets like tigers in a jungle, and fish with horns and quills glowered at them. They saw wonders of the deep which no human eye has ever beheld—but nowhere could they find so much as one clue to the whereabouts of Monstro, the Terror of the Deep.

"The time is getting short!" said Pinocchio at last. "We must find him! My father will starve to death!"

"Father," he cried desperately. But there was no sound except the constant shifting and sighing of the watery depths.

"Let's go home, Pinocchio," Jiminy pleaded. "We'll never find Monstro in this big place. For all we know, we may be looking in the wrong ocean."

"No, Jiminy," said Pinocchio, "I'll never give up! Never!"

Not far away lay the Terror of the Deep, floating close to the surface, fast asleep. At times his broad back rose out of the water, to be mistaken for a desert island.

It was lucky for any ship close by that Monstro

slept, for with but one flip of his tail he had been known to crush the sturdiest craft. As he snored the roars sounded like a tempest. It seemed impossible that anything could live within those crushing jaws.

Yet at the far end of the long, dark cavern formed by the whale's mouth lived a strange household: A kindly old man, whose skin was as pale as white paper, a small black kitten, whose ribs nearly pierced his fur, and a tiny, frightened goldfish, who swam weakly around in her bowl.

The old wood-carver had constructed a rude home, furnished with broken packing cases from ships the whale had swallowed. He had salvaged a lantern, pots and pans, and a few other necessities of life. But his stock of food was now very low; the lantern sputtering above his table was almost out of oil. The end was near.

Every day he fished in the mouth of the whale; but when Monstro slept, nothing entered that dark cavern. Now there was only a shallow pool of water, and it was useless to fish.

"Not a bite for days, Figaro," Geppetto said. "If Monstro doesn't wake up soon, it will be too bad for us. I never thought it would end like this!" He sighed mournfully. "Here we are, starving in the belly of a whale. And Pinocchio—poor little Pinocchio!" Geppetto was obliged to raise his thin voice to a shout, to be heard above the whale's snoring.

The old wood-carver looked tired and worn. He had never been so hungry in his whole life. Figaro was hungry, too. He stared greedily at little Cleo, swimming slowly about her bowl.

As Geppetto went wearily back to his fishing, the kitten began to sneak toward Cleo's bowl. But the old man saw him.

"Scat!" shouted Geppetto. "You beast! Shame on you, Figaro, chasing Cleo, after the way I've brought you up!"

The hungry kitten scuttled away to a corner to try to forget the pangs which gnawed him. Just then Geppetto felt a nibble at his line. He pulled it up in great excitement.

"It's a package, Figaro!" he cried. "Maybe it's food. Sausage, or cheese—"

But when the water-soaked package was

unwrapped, it contained only a cookbook! What a grim trick Fate had played!

"Oh, oh," groaned Geppetto. "I am so hungry! If we only had something to cook! Anything—"

He turned the pages, his mouth watering at the pictured recipes. "101 Ways to Cook Fish," he read. Suddenly his eyes were drawn, as if by a magnet, to Cleo. He could almost see the melted butter sizzling! As in a nightmare, he walked toward the goldfish bowl.

But as he started to scoop his little pet out and put her in the frying pan, the old man realized he could never do this thing.

"Dear Cleo," he begged, "forgive me! If we must die, let us die as we have lived—friends through thick and thin!"

It was a solemn moment. All felt that the end was near.

Then the whale moved!

"He's waking up!" cried Geppetto. "He's opening his mouth!"

Monstro gave an upward lunge, and through his jaws rushed a wall of black water. With it came fish—a whole school of fish! Hundreds of them.

"Food!" yelled Geppetto, seizing his pole. "Tuna fish! Oh, Figaro, Cleo—we are saved!"

And he began to pull fish after fish out of the water.

When Monstro woke, opened his eyes, and saw the school of tuna approaching, he threshed the ocean into turmoil for miles around.

Pinocchio noticed every creature in the sea taking flight, but he did not understand the reason until he saw the whale coming toward him. Then he *knew*.

"Monstro!" he shrieked. "Jiminy, swim for your life!" For although he had long been in search of the Terror of the Deep, a mere look at those crushing jaws was enough to make him flee in terror.

But nothing in Monstro's path could escape. He swallowed hundreds of tuna at one gulp. Into that huge maw finally went Pinocchio!

At last, completely satisfied, the whale grunted and settled down in his watery bed for another nap.

"Blubber-mouth!" cried a shrill, small voice. "Let me in!"

It was Jiminy, clinging to an empty bottle, bobbing up and down outside Monstro's jaws, begging to be swallowed, too.

But the whale paid no attention, except to settle farther into the water. The little cricket was left alone, except for a flock of sea gulls, who began to swoop down and peck at him. He raised his umbrella and drove them away, got inside the bottle, and prepared to wait for Pinocchio.

Inside the whale, although Gepetto's bin was already heaped, he was still at work pulling in tuna.

"There's enough food to last us for months," he told Figaro joyfully. "Wait, there's another big one!" He scarcely noticed a shrill little cry of "Father! Father!"

"Pinocchio?" the old man asked himself in wonderment, and turned around. There, standing before him, was his boy! "Pinocchio!" he exclaimed joyfully. "Are my eyes telling me the truth? Are you really my own dear Pinocchio?"

Geppetto was not the only one who was glad. Figaro licked Pinocchio's face, and little Cleo turned somersaults.

"You see, we have all missed you," said Geppetto fondly. "But you're sneezing! You've caught cold, son! You should not have come down here! Sit down and rest! Give me your hat!"

But when Pinocchio's hat was removed, those hated donkey ears popped out into plain sight.

"Pinocchio!" cried Geppetto, shocked. *"Those ears!"*

Pinocchio hung his head in shame. "I've got a tail, too," he admitted sadly. *"Oh, Father!"* And he turned his head away to hide his tears.

"Never mind, son," Geppetto comforted him. "The main thing is that we are all together again."

Pinocchio brightened up. "The *main* thing is to figure out a way to get out of this whale!"

"I've tried everything," said Geppetto hopelessly. "I even built a raft—"

"That's it!" cried Pinocchio. "When he opens his mouth, we'll float out on the raft!"

"Oh, no," argued Geppetto. "When he opens his mouth everything comes in—nothing goes out. Come, we are all hungry—I will cook a fish dinner! Help me build a fire—"

"That's it, Father!" interrupted Pinocchio. "We'll build a great big fire!" And he began to throw into the fire everything he could get his hands on.

"Not the chairs!" warned Geppetto. "What will we sit on?"

"We won't need chairs," shouted Pinocchio. "We'll build a big fire and make Monstro sneeze! When he sneezes, out we go! Hurry—more wood!"

As the fire began to smoke they got the raft ready.

"It won't work, son," Geppetto insisted mournfully.

But before long the whale began to grunt and cough. Suddenly he drew in his breath and gave a monstrous SNEEZE! Out went the raft, past those crushing jaws, into the sea.

The old man clung weakly to a board. He knew he could never reach land, but there was still hope for Pinocchio.

"Save yourself, my boy!" cried Geppetto. "Swim for shore, and don't worry about me!"

But the brave puppet swam to his father and managed to keep him afloat. Giant waves swept them toward the dark, forbidding rocks which lined the shore. Even if they escaped Monstro, they would surely be crushed to death.

But between two of the rocks there was a small, hidden crevice. By some miracle, Pinocchio and Geppetto were washed through this crevice into a small, sheltered lagoon. Again and again the furious whale threw his bulk against the rocks on the other side. His quarry had escaped!

But alas, when Geppetto sat up dizzily, he saw poor Pinocchio lying motionless beside him, still and pale. The heartbroken old man knelt and wept bitterly, certain his wooden boy was dead.

"We made it!" shouted Pinocchio. "Father, we're free!"

But they were not yet free. The angry whale saw them and plunged ferociously after their frail raft. He hit it squarely, splintering it into thousands of pieces. Pinocchio and Geppetto swam for their lives, with Monstro, the Terror of the Deep, in full pursuit.

The gentle waves carried a fishbowl up onto the beach. It was Cleo—and to the edge of the bowl clung a bedraggled kitten, Figaro. But even they were no comfort to Geppetto now.

A bottle bobbed up out of the water. Inside it rode Jiminy Cricket. He saw what had happened and longed to comfort Geppetto, but his own heart was broken.

The sorrowful old man finally gathered poor

Pinocchio in his arms, picked up his pets, and started home. They too felt sad, for they knew Geppetto was lonelier than he had ever been before.

When they reached home, it no longer seemed a home; it was dark and cheerless. Geppetto put Pinocchio on the workbench, buried his face in his hands, and prayed.

Suddenly a ray of starlight pierced the gloom. It sought out the lifeless figure of the puppet. A voice which seemed to come from the sky said, as it had said once before:

"—and some day, when you have proven yourself brave, truthful, and unselfish, you will be a real boy—"

The old man saw and heard nothing. But Pinocchio stirred, sat up, and looked around. He saw the others grieving, and wondered why. Then he looked down at himself, felt his arms and legs, and suddenly he realized what had happened.

"Father!" he cried. "Father, look at me!"

Pinocchio was alive—really alive. No longer a wooden puppet, but a real flesh-and-blood boy!

Geppetto stared unbelievingly. Once more he picked Pinocchio up in his arms and hugged him, and cried—this time for joy. Again a miracle had been performed; this was truly the answer to his wish—the son he had always wanted!

What did they do to celebrate? Geppetto made a fire and soon the house was as warm and cozy as ever. He started all the clocks and played the music box. Figaro turned somersaults, and Cleo raced madly about her bowl. Pinocchio flew to get his precious toys; even they seemed gayer than ever.

As for Jiminy Cricket, he was the happiest and proudest of all. For on his lapel he now wore a beautiful badge of shining gold!